DESTINY BLOCKERS

AND HOW TO DEMOLISH THEM

JO NAUGHTON

Grosvenor House
Publishing Limited

The right of Jo Naughton to be identified as the author of this
work has been asserted in accordance with Section 78
of the Copyright, Designs and Patents Act 1988

The book cover is copyright to Jo Naughton

This book is published by
Grosvenor House Publishing Ltd
Link House
140 The Broadway, Tolworth, Surrey, KT6 7HT.
www.grosvenorhousepublishing.co.uk

A CIP record for this book
is available from the British Library

ISBN 978-1-80381-424-7
eBook ISBN 978-1-80381-425-4

Some names and details have been changed to protect the
identity of the people whose stories are included in this book.
Bible references are from the New King James Version unless
otherwise stated. The Message and TPT are used to help
reveal the heart of certain passages.

*This book is dedicated to two of the greatest gifts that
God has given to my husband and me. Benj and Abby,
you are wise beyond your years, you are oh so
thoughtful, honorable, incredibly loving, and always forgiving.
I cannot adequately express my gratitude to God for you both.
I am so proud of the way you love Jesus and
pursue your healing so that you can fulfill your destiny.
And thank you for helping me in numerous
ways in this precious ministry. You are the best children
I could have ever asked for, and I love you both very much.*

Acknowledgements

Paolo, thank you for being the best husband, mentor, leader, and encourager I could ever have asked for. Thank you for loving me enough to uncover the issues that were holding me back.

Prophet Nana, thank you for being a powerful example of mountain-moving faith and relentless determination. Thank you for your constant support which has undergirded me through many seasons.

Bishop and Sunny, thank you for your wonderful love, your great friendship, and your phenomenal wisdom. Thank you for being my family when Paul, Benj, and Abby are thousands of miles away.

Freisa, your creativity is phenomenal! Thank you for helping me every step of the way to communicate powerfully with pictures and new ideas.

Contents

HOW TO GET THE MOST OUT OF DESTINY BLOCKERS

As you read Destiny Blockers, search for yourself in its pages. Try to identify which sections paint a picture of your life. You may recognize your reflection throughout. By God's grace, Destiny Blockers will show you some of the obstacles that have been holding you back. I am amazed how often God has a different perspective to mine about my life and my ways. I think my heart is well, but the Lord sees deep within. He knows the truth. Ask the Holy Spirit to show you why you are the way you are, ask Him to reveal hidden hurts so that He can set you free to be your best. I suggest you create a quiet space to read alone. The Spirit of the Lord is ready to take you on a wonderful journey to healing and freedom that will propel you into your God-given purpose.

Chapter One

DELAY AND DERAILMENT

"I'll destroy you. I'll destroy every bone in your body!" Pete yelled down the street as I ran in fear from his home. But I was back the following day. Trapped in a destructive relationship, I was desperate to escape. It all started at college. The evening we met, Pete told me that his faith in God was a pillar in his life. Although I knew deep down that something was wrong, I allowed his words to lull me into a false sense of security. I was dazzled by Pete's confidence and charisma. He had a phenomenal singing voice that gave me goose bumps, and I enjoyed the fact that he was playing the lead role in the college musical. When I was behaving the way he wanted, he made me feel like I was the center of his universe.

Although I was saved when I arrived at the university, I had very little self-worth. I read rejection into almost everything, and craved approval. I longed to be loved and hankered after attention. I hated being alone. The devil sent Pete to meet my warped needs. Looking back over my life, the five years that I was in and out of that relationship were my darkest days. I was lonely and afraid but fed on Pete's attention. One dreadful evening, I remember crying bitterly. I had no idea how to break free, and I was terrified that I would one day marry Pete. No matter how many times I tried to leave, I would find myself back where I started. His accusations and outbursts paralyzed me. I was trapped. Fear would have destroyed my destiny, if not for God, and a deep desire to fulfill the Lord's purposes for my life.

That was many years ago, but the damage done followed me into marriage and even ministry. The remnants of self-worth that I once had were crushed. Although I was serving God, buried pain made me over-sensitive. I felt the need to succeed to prove my value but thought that was just my personality. I was intimidated by strong characters at work and in church, I craved approval and wanted to be the center of attention. Many dreams burned inside, but my God-given gifts were trapped in my heart. On the surface, I looked like a successful Christian woman but, unbeknown to me, hidden issues were blocking my destiny.

Your Heart Decides

I don't know what you have been through, but I do know that you have probably had your fair share of pain and difficulty. Maybe you have suffered far too much. Just as stress can cause physical issues, buried pain can lead to heart problems. Knowing this, the enemy uses the storms of your life to cause destiny-blocking heart diseases. He is a cruel thief, and he is after your promises, he is the arch purpose-blocker. Whether or not you understand the call on your life, the devil will try to delay – or even destroy – your destiny. He knows the Bible and understands that your heart decides the course of your life. Proverbs 4:23 (NIV) says, "Above all else, guard your heart, for everything you do flows from it." Satan targets your heart in an attempt to prevent you from fulfilling your purpose.

Your future is bright. God has planted great dreams inside because He knows you are capable – you are made in His image! He has more than you could imagine in store for you. But He will only open exciting new doors when you are ready to walk through them. In making decisions about your life, God does not consult your résumé. He does not check your skillset or your work experience. Hard work and training are vital, but they are not on the Lord's mind.

Jeremiah 17:10 (NIV) says, "I the Lord search the heart and examine the mind, to reward each person according to their conduct, according to what their deeds deserve." Your Heavenly Father wants to reward you, so He searches your heart to determine if you are ready. He considers the deep issues of your soul when He decides which doors to open. Listen to the same verse in the Message: "But I, God, search the heart and examine the mind. I get to the heart of the human. I get to the root of things. I treat them as they really are, not as they pretend to be." (Jeremiah 17:10 MSG) The enemy knows this Scripture, too, which is why he targets your heart in an attempt to block your progress.

When the Lord was looking for a man to lead His people, He considered the state of the hearts of the candidates. 1 Samuel 16:7 says, "But the Lord said to Samuel, 'Do not look at his appearance or at his physical stature, because I have refused him. For the Lord does not see as man sees; for man looks at the outward appearance, but the Lord looks at the heart.'" Are you believing for a new job or a well-deserved promotion? Are you praying for a breakthrough in your ministry? Do you long to see your business take off? The same God who searched the souls of His people when He chose a new king, is looking at your heart.

After the resurrection of Jesus, the Apostles wanted to appoint a man to replace Judas as the twelfth member of the team. Acts 1:24 (AMP) says, "And they prayed and said, 'You, Lord, Who know all hearts (their thoughts, passions, desires, appetites, purposes, and endeavors), indicate to us which one of these two You have chosen.'" The men who spent three years with Jesus understood God's decision-making process. They asked the Lord which man had the right heart to be appointed as a foundational apostle. The same God who knew the inner workings of these men knows the depths of our hearts, too.

Let's Value What God Values

Almost everything has a price. Basic necessities such as food, phones, clothes, and shoes, all come at a cost. You have to pay for a place to live, a car to drive, or a bike to ride. You have to cough up to fill up with gas, go out for a meal, or go on vacation. The price you are willing to pay demonstrates the value you place on something. If you believe knowledge is important, you will be willing to pay for education. If you value your marriage, you will invest time and effort into your relationship with your spouse.

Stop right now and think about where you invest most of your time and money. Check your calendar and your bank account if you aren't sure. You invest your resources into the things that you consider to be most important. Do you place sufficient value on your heart? There is no point furiously knocking on destiny doors in the hope that one will open if your heart is weighed down and weary. It is time to prioritize your soul for the sake of your future. We are going to look at several reasons why your heart is so important.

You Reflect The Lord

Genesis 1:27 (AMP) says, "So God created man in His own image, in the image and likeness of God He created him; male and female He created them." We do not know much from Scripture about the Lord's physical appearance. We know most about His heart because that is what is most important to God, and your heart was made in the image of your Heavenly Father's heart. But your heart is also unique. Psalms 33:15a says, "He fashions their hearts individually..." We read in Proverbs 27:19 (TPT) that, "Just as no two faces are exactly alike, so every heart is different." Your heart is made in the image of God's heart and yet your heart is unique. No other person has a heart exactly like yours. That means that your heart reflects a distinct part of God's heart. No-one else can reflect our Maker the way you can. As you are healed of the wear and tear of life, you will be able to reflect Him in a wonderful way.

Your heart was formed by the Lord for the giving and receiving of love; it was created for fellowship with your Heavenly Father. As a result, your heart was designed to be absorbent, so that it could soak up His affirming love. It was not made to carry hurts. It was not created to house pain. If you have ever wondered why you are sensitive, even to seemingly insignificant knocks, this could be the reason. Your heart was shaped to take in the atmosphere around you because – until Adam and Eve fell – even the air was filled with love and glory.

The Pains And Strains Of Life

When sin came into the world, it damaged our hearts. It opened the door to guilt, shame, dysfunction, and every form of pain. As you read this book, I believe the Lord will reveal old wounds that are still hampering your life. Your soul, which is so valuable, is also extremely vulnerable. When something that was created to absorb love and glory is exposed to rejection or betrayal, the damage can be significant. It would be like planting a palm tree (which is intended for hot climates) in the Arctic. The tree would take a brutal battering, never fulfill its potential, and eventually wither.

We don't need the Bible to inform us that life can be distressing, but it does. Job 5:7 says, "…man is born to trouble…" 'Âmâl', the Hebrew for trouble, means grief, pain, and misery. You may have experienced more than your fair share of all three. Please don't underestimate the impact that this will probably have had on your wellbeing. Buried pain can sink to the bottom of your soul, weighing you down. Unresolved grief can cause hidden sadness and various physical issues. Abuse, betrayal, and cruelty can crush your confidence. It is essential that you seek your healing.

Health & Wellbeing

If your heart affects every area, of course it impacts your health. 3 John 1:2 says, "Beloved, I pray that you may prosper in all things and be in health, just as your soul prospers." Here we see a direct link between your soul and your health. Inner issues can open the door to physical problems. At the same time, restoration can pave the way for physical healing. I have witnessed many spontaneous miracles at the altar at our events while people were being healed of inner hurts. Joint, bone, and back problems, blood issues, skin diseases, and heart problems have all been healed while God was restoring the souls of His children.

Proverbs 17:22 (TPT) reiterates this: "A joyful, cheerful heart brings healing to both body and soul. But the one whose heart is crushed struggles with sickness and depression." That verse starts by stating that your heart can bring healing to your body. Conversely, when your heart is weighed down, it will impact your wellbeing. You may catch every cold doing the rounds or struggle with problems in your joints. Many times, we look to doctors to solve physical problems that could be permanently resolved through the restoration of the soul.

Certain heart issues can shorten the length of our lives. Proverbs 28:16b says, "...he who hates covetousness will prolong his days." If hating covetousness lengthens our lives, then craving something that belongs to someone else can open the door to an early death. This is such an important correlation that the Lord repeats Himself. Proverbs 14:30 (NLT) explains, "A peaceful heart leads to a healthy body; jealousy is like cancer in the bones." Arthritis ran in my family for years so, as well as dealing with any generational issues, I have had to watch my heart in order to protect my body. This same verse in one of the most literal translations of the Bible puts this principle this way: "A healed heart [is] life to the flesh, And rottenness to the bones [is] envy." (Proverbs 14:30 YLT). Let's deal with our hearts so that we can enjoy the life Jesus died to provide.

One of the Ten Commandments also affects our longevity: "Honor your father and your mother, as the Lord your God has commanded you, that your days may be long, and that it may be

well with you in the land which the Lord your God is giving you."
(Deuteronomy 5:16) If honoring my parents protects my life, then
dishonor may open the door to disease. We must not underestimate
the impact that soul wounds can have on our physical health and
wellbeing. Proverbs 4:20-22 says, "My son, give attention to my
words; incline your ear to my sayings, Do not let them depart
from your eyes; keep them in the midst of your heart; for they are
life to those who find them, and health to all their flesh." I believe
that the Bible truths contained in the pages of this book have the
power to bring healing to your body as well as your soul.

Success In Life And Relationships

Your heart affects every area of your life and impacts all your
relationships. Proverbs 4:23 (NLT) says, "Guard your heart above
all else, for it determines the course of your life." Your heart
decides how your life turns out. It determines whether or not you
fulfill your destiny. This Scripture in the Passion Translation puts
it this way, "So above all, guard the affections of your heart, for
they affect all that you are. Pay attention to the welfare of your
innermost being, for from there flows the wellspring of life."
(Proverbs 4:23 TPT). Your heart affects all that you are, it is the
source of your life. Proverbs 27:19b (NIV) explains that a person's
"...life reflects the heart." Nothing matters more.

Let's look again at 3 John 1:2: "Beloved, I pray that you may
prosper in all things and be in health, just as your soul prospers."
Please notice that the Lord addresses you in this verse as His
"Beloved". The Greek word, agapētos, means dearly loved and
worthy of love. Your Heavenly Father counts you to be worthy of
His love. That is how precious you are to Him. God then shares
His desire to see you succeed in every area of your life. Just as any
loving parent would want their children to do well, the Lord
wants you to live life to the full. John 10:10b (NLT) says, "My
purpose is to give them a rich and satisfying life." God wants you
to thrive in your relationship with Him, in family and friendships,

at work, in business, in ministry, and education, He wants you to prosper in all things. But there is a caveat. 3 John 1:2 explains, "Beloved, I pray that you may prosper in all things and be in health, just as your soul prospers." He wants you to succeed – to the extent that your heart is prospering.

Remember, when God was hunting for someone to promote in Israel, He did not check the candidates' work experience or talents, He considered the state of each person's heart. It was David's inner life that impressed the Lord. Jesus is the same yesterday, today, and forever (see Hebrews 13:8). When He is deciding if you are ready to step into your destiny, He considers your heart. Buried pain or nagging issues can delay or derail the promises of God. He wants to reveal then heal hidden hurts and cleanse you from within so that you are free to succeed.

A River Of Issues

Let's go back to Proverbs 4:23: "Keep your heart with all diligence, for out of it spring the issues of life." The human heart is a river of issues. The issues that I have contended with include comparison and entitlement. Comparison made me feel inferior, but it also caused me to contend with friends to be the best. Entitlement made me easily disappointed and caused me to expect special concessions. All of that was exhausting to me and everyone around me, but I didn't even know that I was bound. The Bible word 'issue' is from a Hebrew root which means a swarm or mass of minute animals. That's exactly what the issues of the heart are like. The word for issue is the same as the word for discharge, and this is what issues are like – unpleasant discharges that can fester and infect.

In the book of Leviticus, when God was telling the Israelites how to keep a healthy, happy community, He talked about people with issues: "And this is his uncleanness in regard to his issue – whether his body runs with his issue or whether his body is stopped up by his issue, it is uncleanness in him." (Leviticus 15:3) Some people 'run' – they eat, sleep, and talk their issues. Being around such people – those who are constantly comparing themselves or driven by the need to please people – can be a drain. They are unwittingly spouting forth their issues and they need help. I was like that at one time, and I am eternally grateful to the people around me for their patience and love.

Others are 'stopped up' or more controlled; their issues are hidden or buried. They conceal how they really feel. Either way, issues affect us – and others. What's inside always finds its way out. If there's junk inside, it'll defile you (and others). The passage in Leviticus says that our issues or discharges make us unclean. Whether it's judgmental thoughts, offense or bitterness, our inner issues defile us. "It's not what goes into your body that defiles you; you are defiled by what comes from your heart... It is what comes from inside you that defiles you." (Mark 7: 14, 20 NLT)

If a fleeting envious thought takes root in your soul, soon that envy will start to infect your attitudes towards that person. Imagine that thought was about someone you love, an encourager. With a small amount of hardness now festering inside, you may find yourself being abrupt or a little resentful. What started out as a tempting thought took root in your heart and wound up defiling you and damaging a relationship. The Leviticus verse goes on to say that whatever a person with an issue touches is defiled. If we don't deal with the matters of our hearts, they come with us everywhere we go, affect all our relationships, and join us in every meeting we attend. So why not take the time to find out what's lurking beneath the surface? Let's pray.

Heavenly Father,

I am determined to fulfill my purpose and use every ounce of my potential, so I ask You to start a new work in my life. I recognize that my heart decides how my life turns out. Will You search my heart, will You shine Your light into the depths of my innermost being? Please reveal any inner issues that are preventing me from achieving my potential. Uncover hidden hurts that are holding me back. Take me on a journey to healing and freedom. Transform me from the inside out so that my life may bring You glory.

In Jesus' name I pray,

Amen.

Chapter Two

I FEEL LIKE A FAILURE

Do you look at the achievements of others and feel like you're not enough? Do you compare your looks or your figure and feel unattractive? Maybe you hear about your friend's grades in school and try to change the topic of conversation. It could be a co-worker's car, house or even family that makes you look at your life and cringe. "He is way better than me." "I'll never be as successful as her." "Why can't I get promoted?" "I feel like a complete failure compared to him." Do you ever think thoughts like those?

Your view of yourself places an invisible ceiling over your potential. However hard you try, however much you pray, if you feel inferior to the people around you, you will probably struggle to make lasting progress. Wonderful opportunities may knock at your door, but if you think others are better than you, you could eventually find yourself back where you started. Your success is connected to the wellbeing of your soul. A sense of inadequacy creates a boundary that is almost impossible to cross. The enemy wants you to feel like a fraud. Comparing yourself with other people is a sure way to squash your self-worth.

Social media can make life tough. Five minutes of browsing can bombard you with everyone else's accomplishments making you painfully aware of your inadequacies. Perhaps it is the workplace that is difficult for you. When your colleague wins contracts or gains recognition, it might make you feel small. You could struggle at church. You look around and assume that everyone else is more spiritual or knowledgeable. Perhaps you watch friends being offered opportunities while your gifts go unnoticed. The devil works overtime to draw you into making comparisons because he knows the damage it does.

The Truth Of The Matter

You were individually designed by the Master Potter, then He threw away the blueprint. No-one else thinks like you, no-one else feels what you do. You are one of a kind. There are no two people in the world who are identical. Of the billions of men and women who have lived and died, no individual has had the same fingerprints as another. There are no duplicates, and there never will be. So, comparing yourself with someone who is different makes no sense. And yet it is a cruel trap that prevents many from fulfilling their purpose.

Comparison feeds some debilitating heart issues. We've already seen how it can make you question your worth, but that's not all. A friend's promotion could make you feel like a failure. Your brother's business taking off may make you embarrassed of your slow start. Hearing about the rapid growth of a church down the road could make you think that your ministry is inferior. Comparison can also lead to anger, self-pity, and jealousy. That's why the enemy wants you to constantly compare yourself.

Paul the Apostle wrote in 2 Corinthians 10:12: "For we dare not class ourselves or compare ourselves with those who commend themselves. But they, measuring themselves by themselves, and comparing themselves among themselves, are not wise." As you read this chapter, I believe that the Lord will reveal unhealthy habits that have been holding you back. Comparison might be a huge issue, or it may be a subtle problem.

You could constantly look over your shoulder and feel small. If that's you, ask the Lord to show you where this sense of inadequacy came from. Was it a teacher? A sibling? A parent? The Lord wants to reveal unhealed hurts deep down that have made you believe that you are less valuable than other people. He will heal the wounds that have made you susceptible to looking down on yourself. Alternatively, comparison could be an occasional issue that blindsides you every now and then. I am going to lead you in prayer, then I encourage you to take a few moments to complete the self-assessment below.

Heavenly Father,

I open up to You and I ask You to search my heart. I pray that You would reveal any unhealthy habits and show me the underlying causes. Shine Your light into the depths of my soul and show me any issues that have been holding me back.

In Jesus' name I pray,

Amen.

Your Thoughts

How often do you have thoughts similar to those that follow?

Mark either hourly, daily, weekly, monthly, or never, on the right-hand side.

1. She's prettier or thinner than me   _____

2. I'll never do as well as him   _____

3. I'm a failure compared to her   _____

4. He has achieved so much more than me   _____

5. I'll never be as successful as her   _____

6. Compared to him, I'm embarrassed of myself   _____

7. She is way more spiritual than me   _____

8. I don't know anything compared to him   _____

Any thoughts marked monthly are not a big deal, but still need to be stamped out of your life. More frequent responses indicate that this is an issue you need to tackle for the sake of your destiny.

Blind Spots

Note down five settings you often visit. Your list might include work, church, home, the gym, social media, college, Bible study, social gatherings, and so on. Then score your propensity to compare yourself with other people in that environment on a scale of 1 (highly unlikely) to 5 (highly likely).

Environments   **Comparison Rating**

1) _____   _____

2) _____   _____

3) _____   _____

4) _____   _____

5) _____   _____

Any score of 3 or more is a red flag and an area that you need to address. Irrespective of which end of the spectrum you are on, let's go on a journey to freedom.

A Generation Cheated

Numbers tells the tragic story of how an entire generation missed God's promises. Israel's best leaders were chosen to explore the land that God had pledged to His people. These could not have been novices; they must have been mature and experienced men. I would imagine that Moses picked them for their bravery and spirituality. Twelve men went to the Promised Land to get a feel for the terrain so that they could help plan the conquest. Instead of focusing on the mission and the size of their God, ten of these leaders compared themselves with the local people. They felt inadequate and told their countrymen that they could not conquer Canaan. The people of Israel believed these ten leaders and sealed their fate in the desert.

Numbers 13:31-33 says, "But the men who had gone up with him said, 'We are not able to go up against the people, for they are stronger than we.' And they gave the children of Israel a bad report of the land which they had spied out, saying, 'The land through which we have gone as spies is a land that devours its inhabitants, and all the people whom we saw in it are men of great stature. There we saw the giants (the descendants of Anak came from the giants); and we were like grasshoppers in our own sight, and so we were in their sight.'"

Fake News

Let's use this passage to expose what happens when we make comparisons. The ten made assumptions about the strength of their opponents. I am certain they did not create a competition to assess the power of these people. They *presumed* that the residents were better warriors. Comparison pushes us to make assumptions. It will tell you that other people are stronger, smarter, or more successful than they really are. It will exaggerate the gifts and talents of others and it will minimize your qualities. It broadcasts fake news. When you listen to the whispers of comparison, you are listening to lies. The descending spiral into self-loathing can be crushing.

In John 8:44b (AMP), Jesus describes the devil: "...When he speaks a falsehood, he speaks what is natural to him, for he is a liar [himself] and the father of lies and of all that is false." If the devil can get you to focus on the people around you, he knows he can feed you fake news. And this false information is designed to cause doubt and discouragement. It is intended to squash your confidence. The men of Israel probably went out full of faith.

15

They will have been excited about seeing their future homeland. But once they focused on the abilities of the competition, their courage evaporated and fear entered their hearts.

Maybe you were planning to apply for a job and you knew that you had a shot. However, when you heard about the other candidate's experience, you doubted your ability and withdrew your application. Perhaps you were in a wonderful relationship but you worried that you weren't good enough. You built walls around your heart to avoid being hurt and ended up sabotaging your own happiness. Let me repeat myself: comparison opens the door to doubt and discouragement, and it crushes confidence.

The Thing About Confidence

To thrive in the midst of life's ups and downs and to fulfill our potential, we need confidence. The way that it is usually developed in the heart of a child is through the affirming words of their parents or caregivers. But if reassurance is inadequate or missing, life's difficulties can strip even a strong soul of security. One of the most significant words I received was spoken over me at Bible College. I can't remember the topic being taught that day or why I had gone to the front of the auditorium for prayer. However, I will never forget what the Dean of Students pronounced as he prayed over me: "You're too small! You're too small in your own eyes." I can still hear those words like it was yesterday. I didn't believe in myself, and until I did, many of God's plans were put on hold.

Lack of confidence usually looks inwardly at our inadequacy. However, the Creator of heaven and earth is with *you*. He not only loves you, He believes in you. He has confidence in you even when you lack confidence in yourself. Where others have dismissed you out of hand, He gives you His vote. Where others have doubted your worth, He has faith in you. When you put your trust in Him, He will not allow you to be put to shame. He will protect you. Joshua 1:5 (MSG) says, "I'll be with you. I won't give up on you; I won't leave you." You have the Lord Of All on your side.

16

Hebrews 10:35 says, "Therefore do not cast away your confidence, which has great reward." Confidence gives you the courage to step out in faith, and it is rewarded. When the ten spies concentrated on their opponents' strength, their confidence evaporated. They felt insignificant. The devil wants you too to focus on the talents of others, but it's a trap.

Why Did They Look Down On Themselves?

Have you ever wondered *why* these men looked down on themselves? Why were they susceptible to self-doubt? Why was it so easy for them to believe that their enemies were better than them? If you have read any of my other books, or if you're part of Jo's Mentoring Network, you have probably heard me make reference to 'Rebekah's Request'. Rebekah was married to Abraham's son Isaac, and her story is told in the book of Genesis. She asked God a critical question. In my view, it is one of the most insightful and pivotal prayers in Scripture.

After years of believing God for a baby, Isaac and Rebekah discovered they were going to be parents. No doubt they were overjoyed. However, as the pregnancy progressed, something felt wrong. We don't know whether she was in pain or if she was just unsettled. Whatever was going on inside, it didn't feel right, so Rebekah inquired of the Lord, "If all is well, why am I like this?" (Genesis 25:22b). The Lord revealed the reason for her rumblings: she was carrying twins with conflicting destinies.

I cannot tell you how many times I have prayed that prayer. Any time my reactions to daily situations don't add up or make sense, I go to God and ask, "If all is well, then why am I like this?" If a passing comment hurts my feelings or if correction feels like rejection, I ask God to reveal the reason. If someone disrespects me and it makes me feel small, I ask God to uncover the cause. The measuring line is easy to establish. If Jesus would respond differently to the way I have reacted to life's knocks, then that tells me there is something amiss in my heart.

The Scars Of Suffering

Why would God's chosen people feel inferior to His enemies? I believe the reason is that they were raised in slavery. These men were treated like animals by their 'owners'. Forced to work long hours in blazing temperatures by cruel masters, every beating will have bruised their hearts as much as their flesh. Cruelty is degrading. It tells its victims that they are worthless. I imagine that these men struggled to believe in themselves because they still believed the lies that their suffering had whispered. Let's look at why painful experiences can lead us to believe filthy lies.

Firstly, circumstances speak. The car refusing to start may say the day will be tough. A spilled coffee might tell you that you're clumsy. Bad weather on your birthday could suggest the year will be difficult. The events of your life talk. Do you remember the story of the fig tree that withered? Jesus was hungry and saw a fig tree in the distance, covered with leaves, and hoped to find some fruit to eat. However, when He looked closely, He found nothing but leaves. Mark 11:14 (KJV) says, "And Jesus answered and said unto it, 'No man eat fruit of thee hereafter for ever.' And his disciples heard it." Jesus *answered* the tree, which means that it was speaking to Him.

When things go wrong, the pain you suffer tells you a story. If you have suffered a great deal, the difficulties you have endured will probably have whispered cruel lies to your heart. Maybe repeated rejection has made you believe that you don't deserve to be loved. Perhaps it has told you that you are not good enough. I believe that the cruelty of slavery spoke to these men. It told them that they had no value. So, when they looked at the power of their opponents, they saw themselves as incapable.

Which Lies Do You Believe?

Deep down, you may think that you were bullied *because* you were weak. You could believe that you were ridiculed *because* you

18

are dumb. Proverbs 23:7 says, "For as he thinks in his heart, so is he..." The Hebrew for 'thinks' in this verse is 'šâ'ar', which means to estimate or to calculate. When things happen to us, we make unconscious calculations about ourselves. If you were rejected, the pain of being pushed away may have caused you to make assumptions about your value. You may have concluded that you are not worthy of love. If you were humiliated, you may have decided that you are stupid. If you were abused, you could have ended up believing that you are dirty or cheap. Cruelty is so crushing that is causes you to believe lies about yourself. When the Lord heals your heart, it becomes easier to dismiss the devil's fake news.

Ecclesiastes 7:7 says, "Surely oppression destroys a wise man's reason..." Oppression in the Hebrew is 'šeq', which means injury, distress or cruelty. Reason is 'hâlal' which means to shine. This verse powerfully describes the impact of cruelty. It blots out your shine. If you have lost your sparkle, check your heart for unresolved hurts. Have you had the fire in your soul extinguished by pain? Proverbs 15:13 (NLT) explains, "A glad heart makes a happy face; a broken heart crushes the spirit." Relationship breakdown, loss of a loved one, or cruelty, could have severely wounded your soul.

The Message version of Ecclesiastes 7:7 says, "Brutality... destroys the strongest heart." Cruelty damages your self-worth, dims the light that shines from within, and the pain it leaves behind weighs you down. Please don't ignore your inner wellbeing; it determines the course of your life. Ask the Lord to restore you from the inside out. I will lead you in prayer for healing at the end of this section. I promise you, there is no heartache that the Lord can't heal.

Your Interpreter

If you believe a lie, then you will interpret everything that happens through the lens of that falsehood. Painful experiences of the past can cause you to wrongly interpret the words or actions of family or friends. Our two-day course 'Healed for Life' is translated from English into Spanish. During one session, I was sharing with brutal honesty about some old issues in my marriage. I explained that the most important moment was when I faced the truth. I stopped blaming my husband for our problems and recognized that my shortcomings were the cause of our issues.

Somehow the interpreter did not catch what I said. My interpreter had said that the root of our problems was that my husband was a womanizer! I cleared up the mistake, we all roared with laughter, and I carried on. What is my point? The Spanish speakers believed that the interpreter was telling the truth – until we cleared up the misunderstanding. It was the only version of the story that they could hear. It is the same for you and me. We believe our inner interpreter is presenting an accurate account of events. We take what it says as gospel.

If you've been pushed away or put down throughout your life, you may read rejection into your daily interactions. Criticism, abrupt answers, or closed doors may make you feel unwanted. If you've been betrayed in your marriage, you may be suspicious of even the slightest sign of a wandering heart. We interpret what's happening today in the light of what we suffered yesterday. That is, until we are healed of our deep hurts.

Reading Wrongly

We learn in the Gospels about a storm that broke out on the Sea of Galilee. Mark 4:37-38 (AMP) says, "And a furious storm of wind [of hurricane proportions] arose, and the waves kept beating into the boat, so that it was already becoming filled. But He [Himself] was in the stern [of the boat], asleep on the [leather] cushion; and they awoke Him and said to Him, 'Master, do You not care that we are perishing?'"

The disciples assumed that Jesus did not care about them because He was sleeping. They wrongly interpreted His peace as

20

indifference. Jesus' closest friends believed that the Lord didn't care about them, and for a moment their assumptions would have made them feel unloved. Their interpretation made them feel hurt and wronged. Sometimes we are wounded by our interpretations rather than by what's actually happening.

Let's go back to the story of the men who went to check out the Promised Land. The pain of their slavery-bound past made them believe the lie that they were small and insignificant. When they saw the strength of the local people, they were intimidated and they compared themselves. They forgot God's word to them and concluded that they were incapable of winning a battle. They wrongly read the situation, and it cost them their happiness and prosperity.

If you often feel inferior, it's time to ask why. Why do you think other people are better than you? Why do you feel like a fraud? When you look into the mirror, what do you see? Do you see a champion? Do you see someone who is destined for greatness? Do you see someone who is made in the image and likeness of our awesome God? Or do you see a second-rate human being? Do you see a failure? Do you see a man or woman who has been marked by rejection? When you look deep inside, what do you see?

The Lord wants to heal the hurts that have made you believe that you are less valuable. That's the first step towards breaking free from this destiny blocker. After that, it will be easier to change your behavior so that you stop making unhealthy comparisons.

A Cruel Trap

Israel's finest destroyed their futures. They compared themselves with their opponents and doubted their abilities. Comparison takes your eyes off God's promises, it removes your attention from your Way Maker, and it focuses your thoughts on someone who is different. If you suffer from any sense of inadequacy, then all the devil must do to get you down is to show you someone else's success. The father of lies will try to convince you that the person you are looking at is smarter, stronger, and more successful than you will ever be. Even while you are still on your journey to inner security and wellbeing, you can stop Satan by taking your eyes off others and turning your attention to the Lord.

Hearing a brother share his testimony can create faith that your blessing is coming. God's plan is that the breakthroughs of others will encourage you to pursue your dreams. The Lord longs for you to rejoice at another's victory and see their win as evidence that yours is coming. The enemy tries to skew your perspective. He wants you to hear of the successes of others and feel overshadowed by their 'brilliance'. The devil wants the progress of a friend to make you feel inadequate. Comparison is a destructive response to testimony.

We Can All Get Sucked In

God has called me to lead a movement that brings healing to God's people across the world. We hold conferences and meetings in various countries. On one occasion, as I boarded a ten-hour flight to minister at an event, we had just six bookings! I started thinking about powerful women preachers who attracted huge crowds. Some were younger than me yet making a massive impact. Others had best-selling books and back-to-back bookings to minister at huge conferences. As I compared my effectiveness with theirs, I felt like a joke. Discouragement set in as I wondered what on earth I was doing wrong. My attention was fixed on the success of others, and it was eating away at my faith.

I eventually realized what was happening and pulled my attention away from these wonderful women. Instead, I focused on the faithfulness of my Heavenly Father and thought about how far He had brought us. I reminded myself that Jesus taught us to leave the 99 to help just one. Negativity drained away as I thanked the Lord for the opportunity to bring healing to His people. I promised to give my best, irrespective of how many people showed up. Joy returned.

Galatians 5:26 (MSG) says, "...we will not compare ourselves with each other as if one of us were better and another worse. We have far more interesting things to do with our lives. Each of us is an original." When I compare my job, my children, my ministry, my position, my life, or my gifts, I am straying outside my business. God made me unique, so how can I determine my success or failure by comparing myself with others? It's impossible.

Of course, some measurement is healthy. We rummage through clothes in our favorite shop to find the garment we like the most. We compare prices to find the best deal. But comparison is a problem when it is used as a measure of success; it is dangerous when it is combined with insecurity. In those instances, it can create a breeding ground for other heart problems. Unfortunately, making those sorts of comparisons is a bad habit that has the power to block your destiny.

Pushed Out

Sophie was five when her sister, Rache, was born. Until that time, she had been her mother's only child and the center of her universe. The arrival of Rache made Sophie feel rejected. It's not that her mother had actually pushed her away, but the shock of a newcomer in the house made Sophie feel unwanted. She compared the attention she and Rache were receiving and felt less loved. It was not long before jealousy entered Sophie's heart.

By the time Rache joined her sister at High School, the relationship was fraught with problems. Sophie supposed that Rache was that little bit cleverer, prettier, and more popular than her. She compared herself with her little sister and competed for the spotlight. She put Rache down in front of school friends, reported her mistakes to their parents, and took every opportunity to embarrass or undermine her little sister.

Sophie ruined an important relationship, and feelings of resentment dominated much of her youth. Rache was wounded by her sister's constant put-downs and drifted from her family. She kept a distance from the sibling that had caused her so much hurt. As an adult, Sophie regretted having a sister that she didn't really know. A lifetime of comparison caused dysfunction. Eventually, Sophie faced the truth and asked God to heal the rejection she felt at Rache's birth. She asked for forgiveness of the pain she caused and started on the road to recovery. As adults, Sophie's relationship with Rache began afresh.

It Started At The Very Beginning

The sin of negative comparison began in the Garden of Eden. Satan tempted Eve to compare herself with God. The devil told her that if she ate fruit from the tree of the knowledge of good and evil, she would become like God. God had already made her in His image. She was already like God. Nevertheless, she coveted God's gifting; she focused on what she thought she did not have and ate the forbidden fruit. Eve opened the door for comparison to enter the hearts of the generations to come.

The next to be devastated by comparison were Adam and Eve's sons, Cain and Abel. If God blesses your brother, that doesn't mean He likes you less. The promotion of your sister doesn't mean He won't shower you with His goodness. Yet all too often, people feel threatened by the blessing or success of others. Cain and his younger brother Abel both had a heart to serve the Lord. In fact, Cain was the first to bring an offering to God. He gave some of his crops and fruit, and Abel brought God his first-born lambs.

I believe the Lord had taught the sons of Adam about offerings. Perhaps God had explained the importance of giving your best. I'm sure He was about to teach them more. However, when Cain saw that his brother's gift was better, he became very upset. God knew that Cain was angry so He explained to the young man that if he made the right choices, he would do well. I believe that God had great plans for Cain.

In Genesis 4:7 (NLT), God said, "You will be accepted if you do what is right. But if you refuse to do what is right, then watch out! Sin is crouching at the door, eager to control you. But you must subdue it and be its master." Cain could have calmed his heart and turned his face away from focusing on his brother's blessings. He could have learned from this experience. Instead, he allowed jealousy to turn to hatred, and he killed his brother.

Comparison leads to serious inner issues. If we don't stop it in its tracks, it will cause problems such as discouragement, jealousy, and shame. You probably won't end up committing murder like Cain, but perhaps you are tempted to give up on your dreams or compete with a friend. You may feel left out or unwanted. That's exactly how the enemy plans it.

Favoritism

It can be painful if your father or mother preferred your brother or sister. Unfair treatment at home can wound your heart. We see examples of God's people being affected by favoritism. Jacob grew up knowing his dad adored his twin brother Esau. Consequently, Jacob spent much of his early life trying to prove himself. If you feel the need to prove the value you add, I encourage you to use Rebekah's Request to ask the Lord why. There is a big difference between being motivated and being driven. When you are motivated, you persevere out of the desire to make a difference. When you are driven, your determination is rooted in the need to succeed. Motivation is energizing, whereas drivenness is exhausting. When you are motivated, failing teaches you important lessons. When you are driven, failing makes you feel like a failure.

I believe that Jacob pursued success in an effort to prove his value to his father, and to himself. Knowing that one of your parents preferred your brother or sister can cause a deep root of rejection and turn comparison into a lifelong habit. Jacob probably envied Esau's relationship with their dad. Rejection makes people feel like they are on the outside. Jacob probably felt like an outsider in his own family; maybe you can relate to that pain. Even when we don't want to repeat the mistakes of our parents, we often do, until we are healed of our wounds. Jacob's sons were hurt by his own preferential love for Joseph. They were treated differently to the 'dreamer' and jealousy took root in their hearts. Joseph's brothers probably felt that they were not good enough. Like Cain, they sought to destroy the one who was favored. Rejection can all too easily become a breeding ground for jealousy.

When you have been wounded by favoritism, you are more likely to feel excluded when the spotlight is on someone else. You are more likely to compare yourself with other people and feel inadequate. If a leader or your boss celebrates someone else, it may make you feel forgotten. It's always best to resist the temptation to compare yourself with other people. Remember, you are unique, and you are special to God. If you keep that in mind, it will be easier to rejoice with others in their season of favor.

Competition

God spoke to Abraham in Genesis 12 and promised to make his name great. Abraham's success was not dependent on his rising higher than others. His success was dependent on him becoming *his* best. In the same way, your achievement is not determined by how you measure against other people. The Lord's plan is that every one of us will be great because we are made in the image of the Greatest.

For many exhausting years, I craved attention and recognition. I wanted to be noticed and celebrated. Without people's love and admiration, I felt small and insignificant. If I wasn't comparing myself and feeling inadequate, I would compete with the people around me. I wanted to be more spiritual, more knowledgeable, or more successful. If somebody I thought was on a level with me shone more brightly, I felt overshadowed. I would reach for the spotlight with anecdotes that proved my value. I wanted people to think that I was capable. If peers seemed more important than me, it made me feel small. It was awful. Once God started to heal my heart of all the reasons why I felt I wasn't enough, it became easy to stop striving. It would be my honor to lead you to restoration. After the Lord has begun healing your heart, we will close the chapter of your life marked by comparison. Let's pray:

Heavenly Father,

I open my heart to You and I ask You to shine Your light into hidden hurts that have made me feel inferior. Reveal faults in the foundation of my heart that have made me think that I am less valuable than other people. Uncover the reasons why I compete with friends or family.

(*Now tell the Lord how you feel about yourself, sharing as much detail as possible. Describe any memories that surface. Tell Him what was said or done and how it made you feel. Explain the pain of rejection, cruelty, favoritism, or any other experience that the Holy Spirit brings to the surface. Jesus is your Wonderful Counsellor, so pour out your heart in His presence. Talk to Him openly. Then continue with the prayer below.*)

I ask You to restore my heart, Lord. Take my pain away and fill me with your wonderful healing love. I receive Your acceptance in the depths of my heart. Thank You that I am Your child, I belong to You, and You will never leave me or abandon me. Your love for me is perfect and it will never change. I receive Your wonderful love.

In Jesus' name,

Amen.

A Fresh Start

Your life can be gloriously transformed by changing the way you think. The old way of living led to discouragement and insecurity. It choked your faith and kept you out of God's best. A new mindset will unleash joy in your life and open new doors. Change requires commitment, but the liberty it produces is worth the effort. When I stopped habitually measuring myself against others, it set me free. Of course, we all occasionally make unhealthy comparisons, but once you have a new outlook, you will find it much easier to manage wayward thoughts.

Let's read Romans 12:2b (AMP): "...be transformed (changed) by the [entire] renewal of your mind [by its new ideals and its new attitude], so that you may prove [for yourselves] what is the good and acceptable and perfect will of God, even the thing which is good and acceptable and perfect [in His sight for you]." When you reform your thinking by allowing heaven's values to guide you, you set yourself up to enjoy God's perfect plans. We need to dismantle old assumptions and replace them with the truth.

A value is a principle adopted by an individual or an organization to steer everything they do. If they are implemented correctly, decision-makers would sooner close down than knowingly go against their core principles. It's time for you to adopt some new, non-negotiable values for your life. Any time you realize you are straying away from them, come back to what you know to be right. After a while, these will become your truths. I will articulate them for you as statements that you can make about yourself or declarations that you can speak over your life.

I Am Unique

Science and Scripture are clear: you are unique. Psalms 139:13-14 says, "For You formed my inward parts; You covered me in my mother's womb. I will praise You, for I am fearfully and wonderfully made. Marvelous are Your works, and that my soul knows very well." You were skillfully crafted by the Master Creator who makes no mistakes. He has no 'off days'. Ephesians 2:10 affirms this: "For we are His workmanship, created in Christ Jesus for good works, which God prepared beforehand that we should walk in them."

Every day, when you pray, declare out loud in prayer, "I am fearfully and wonderfully made. I am God's handiwork, and He does all things well. I am unique." If you notice yourself drawn to an unhealthy comparison, take captive that wayward thought and say to yourself, "I will not compare myself with other people because I am unique." Take your eyes off your brother or sister and look to the Lord. Remind yourself of your value to your Heavenly Father.

I Am Enough

The verse I am about to share changed my life. Colossians 2:9-10 says, "For in Him dwells all the fullness of the Godhead bodily; and you are complete in Him..." God is supremely powerful – and you are complete in Him. You and Jesus are a majority, and through your relationship with Him, you are already enough. You are sufficient. Allow that truth to sink deep down. You don't need to strive because you are already enough. You don't need to compete because you're already a success. Your greatness is inbuilt – it comes from your Designer.

The Greek word for grace is 'charis', which literally means favor. 1 Corinthians 15:10 states, "But by the grace of God, I am what I am..." Understanding the meaning of grace, you can accurately interpret this verse as, "...by the favor of God, I am what I am..." It's God's favor that determined your height, your looks, and your abilities. Embrace the person that the Lord designed you to be. There is only one of you on the planet. Please don't try to be like anyone else; be your best with the help of your Heavenly Father.

Add this to your daily declarations: "I am what I am by the favor of God. I am complete in Him and I am already enough." You can be confident in the knowledge that you are enough for your Heavenly Father. Proverbs 3:26 says, "For the Lord will be your confidence..." Take your eyes off other people and focus on God's plan for your life. When you remind yourself of what He says in His word about you, you will be reminded of your value. You will no longer feel the need to look to others to assess your success. As I bring this chapter to a close, we will leave old behaviors behind in prayer and embrace a new way of life. We will close with a final paragraph of declarations. You may want to come back to these statements to speak over yourself daily. Let's pray.

Heavenly Father,

Thank You for Your wonderful love for me and for the great plans that You have for my life. I want to apologize for every time that I have compared myself with other people. You have made me unique. I realize that measuring myself against people who are different to me is both futile and unhelpful. I choose today to give up this unhealthy habit. Holy Spirit, I ask for Your help to stop making comparisons. Any time I accidentally measure myself against someone else, I will take captive that wayward thought. I will move my attention back to You. I will remind myself of Your promises to me.

I embrace a new thought life. When I see the achievements of others, I will celebrate their successes. When I see the talents of others, I will thank God for His goodness. I will remind myself that, by the favor of God, I am what I am. My success is measured by my obedience to Your word, not by the progress of others. I will endeavor to keep my eyes fixed on You, Oh Lord.

I was fearfully and wonderfully made. I am God's handiwork, and He does all things well. I am unique and I am complete in Him. Jesus and I together are a majority. Through my relationship with the Lord, I am already enough. I am sufficient! I give You praise for the things that You have done in my heart and life.

In Jesus' name I pray,

Amen.

Chapter Three

THE OTHER SIDE OF INJUSTICE

Walking out of the hospital, I felt like I was in the middle of an unthinkable dream. Once home, reality hit as I made some terrible telephone calls. Two stuck in my memory like they were yesterday. "Dad, I have some awful news—." "She's not dead?" he interrupted. My father's candor punched my heart as though I was hearing the 'd' word for the first time. Then there was a conversation with a friend. I don't recall how I shared what had happened, but I will never forget her reaction. "NO!" my friend gasped as she collapsed on the floor. Those calls were like a photograph of the brutality of our new reality.

Our bright-eyed, fun-loving little girl was gone. Naomi was running around a mall on Monday, went downhill in the early hours of Tuesday, and died of meningitis on Wednesday morning. The shock was ruthless and our loss indescribable. Naomi was our only child at the time, so my husband and I were also robbed of our role as parents. The Saturday after she passed away, I remember thinking that the sun was cruel to shine so brightly. I was plunged into unimaginable pain and tormented by confusion. My husband and I were doing our best to take care of His family – our small but growing church – yet our family had been torn apart.

There is something about unexpected death that is a bitter assault.1 Samuel 30:6a (AMP) describes how King David and his men felt when they returned home to discover their city in ruins and their families gone: "David was greatly distressed, for the men spoke of stoning him because the souls of them all were bitterly grieved, each man for his sons and daughters..." These mighty warriors were not just in pain. Their families had been taken, their loved ones were gone; they were *bitterly* grieved. Untimely loss is just one example of a crushing life experience that can leave you reeling with pain but also tormented by a sense of injustice.

Perhaps you were abused by someone who should have provided love and protection. You could have been pushed away by the one who promised to love you forever. Maybe a business partner or family member cheated you out of what was rightfully yours, leaving you struggling to survive. Perhaps you were abandoned in your time of need or betrayed by someone you trusted. Maybe you went through some other devastating experience. Such agony can leave you winded by the sheer force of the pain.

Proverbs 1:27 (NIV) says, "When calamity overtakes you like a storm, when disaster sweeps over you like a whirlwind, when distress and trouble overwhelm you." Pain can batter like a storm. It can cause untold distress. As though the hurt alone weren't enough, events like the ones I mentioned should never happen, so the sense of injustice can be terrible. That's when the devil tries to exploit your vulnerability by making everything worse. Let me explain...

The Devil's Plan For Your Pain

After repeated rejection, the enemy wants you to shut down so that he can trap you in isolation. Following betrayal, Satan seeks to shatter trust, making you wary of building relationships. After the agony of injustice, the enemy wants to trap you in torment. Rehearsing conversations or reliving events, you go over every detail, again and again. You may be okay until something or someone reminds you of the wrongs you suffered, and without notice, you are back in that place of pain. Perhaps you cut certain people out of your life and have no desire to ever see them again.

Mention of their names or the thought of their faces could cause upset. Maybe particular phrases remind you of a terrible season, and each time you remember what was said, it hurts again. Let's uncover a terrible destiny blocker that the enemy uses to hurt God's people after the pain of injustice.

The devil is a liar. John 8:44b (AMP) says, "...there is no truth in him. When he speaks a falsehood, he speaks what is natural to him, for he is a liar [himself] and the father of lies and of all that is false." As an expert liar, the enemy knows how to deceive you and me. You see, the devil has something in common with us that he exploits. Jeremiah 17:9 (AMP) says, "The heart is deceitful above all things... Who can know it [perceive, understand, be acquainted with his own heart and mind]?" We think we know ourselves, but all too often, we don't. Put simply, this Scripture says that your soul can, and probably does, lie to you. Your heart will tell you that all is well when deep hurts are hiding inside. Your heart will avoid the truth to escape the pain. Scripture asks a rhetorical question: Who can really know or understand their own heart and mind? The implication is that none of us really knows what is hiding inside.

After the upset associated with injustice, the devil seeks to bury bitterness deep within. He wants to trap you in pain, spoil your relationships, and prevent you from embracing your destiny. You may not think that you are harboring any hidden hurts, but please keep your heart open as you read. We have seen countless testimonies of restoration after devastating loss and betrayal. My prayer for you is that any deep-rooted suffering is uncovered. Once this issue is exposed to the light by the Spirit of God, you can begin your journey to healing and freedom. You will then be ready to rise again and fulfill your highest purpose.

Poisoned Arrows

One time while I was worshiping, the Lord interrupted my song to tell me that I needed to uproot bitterness. I was shocked; I had worked hard to forgive the people involved in a particularly painful season. Almost immediately, certain phrases began replaying in my heart and the Holy Spirit revealed words lodged deep down. God took me to four hurtful statements that still made me feel uncomfortable. I often heard these phrases play out in my thoughts. I realized that I needed to deal with these verbal arrows.

One by one, I told the Lord what was said and why it hurt me. I described the pain that I felt in prayer. I shared how wrong it was and how judged I felt. I cried as I poured out my heart like water before the face of the Lord (see Lamentations 2:19). I hadn't even realized that those comments had cut me to the core. After sharing my pain with my Wonderful Counsellor (see Isaiah 9:6), I forgave the people who spoke those words. I cancelled any debt that I felt they owed me, and I asked the Lord the bless them. After nearly an hour, my heart was free. This encounter was not long ago, and yet I cannot remember all four comments! Words that had once been engraved in my mind were erased. Remember, I had no idea that I was harboring bitterness until the Holy Spirit showed me my heart.

Afterwards, I asked the Lord to help me understand the difference between holding anger against a person and holding onto wounding words. He brought me to Psalms 64:3: "Who sharpen their tongue like a sword, and bend their bows to shoot their arrows – bitter words." Sometimes bitterness is not caused by unfair behavior but by unjust words. The things that people have said can get lodged in the soul.

Long after they were said, bitter words can trouble your peace. Proverbs 12:18a says, "There is one who speaks like the piercings of a sword…" Cruel comments can be as brutal as a knife attack. The Lord wants to heal your heart and cleanse any angst left behind. If you vividly recall unkind or unjust comments, you probably need to ask the Lord to remove the arrows from your heart. Psalms 140:3 (NLT) describes the intensity of verbal attacks:

"Their tongues sting like a snake; the venom of a viper drips from their lips." You need to be healed of the pain and let go of the wrong. We will deal with this at the end of this chapter. This was an example of bitterness hiding in my heart. Perhaps there is some buried in yours.

The Big Problem With Bitterness

The Lord's love is unconditional, it has no boundaries, it is never ending, and it is unchanging. It is that love that motivated God to send His only Son Jesus to die so that you could enjoy life. God loves you, and nothing you do could make Him love you any less, or even any more, because His love for you is perfect. On the other hand, grace, which is God's favor, is conditional. Hebrews 12:15a says, "Looking carefully lest anyone fall short of the grace of God..." This destiny blocker can cause us to fall short of God's grace. This is a serious matter. Ephesians 2:8 (AMP) says, "For it is by free grace (God's unmerited favor) that you are saved (delivered from judgment and made partakers of Christ's salvation) through [your] faith. And this [salvation] is not of yourselves [of your own doing, it came not through your own striving], but it is the gift of God." As the famous hymn goes, 'Amazing Grace, how sweet the sound that saved a wretch like me...' If we are saved by grace, then falling short of His favor is dangerous.

The Greek word translated as grace means favor. The Bible details ways that we can attract God's favor. Jesus grew in favor with God. Luke 2:52 says, "And Jesus increased in wisdom and stature, and in favor with God and men." That means that Jesus enjoyed more favor with God as an adult than He did as a young man. You and I can also attract increasing levels of God's favor through our obedience and faithfulness (see Genesis 6:7-9). However, just as we can increase in favor by doing the right things, we can repel God's favor.

Hebrews 12:14-15 says, "Pursue peace with all people, and holiness, without which no-one will see the Lord: looking carefully lest anyone fall short of the grace of God; lest any root of bitterness springing up cause trouble, and by this many become defiled." This verse reveals three terrible results of this heart issue. Firstly, bitterness can cut us off from God's favor. A pure heart is like a bridge to God's favor; no wonder the devil will do anything to destroy that bridge. Favor opens doors, creates new opportunities, and attracts the goodness of both God and people. Bitterness has the power to hold back favor.

But it doesn't stop there. Hebrews 12:15b reveals a second danger: "...lest any root of bitterness springing up cause trouble, and by this many become defiled." Bitterness contaminates the people around us. If we don't deal with bitterness, we can unwittingly hurt those we love the most. Thirdly, because bitterness is a root, and roots run deep, it can also cause you to get stuck, making lasting progress hard. You may try to move forwards, but you find yourself struggling to leave a traumatic season behind. This is another heart issue that causes sickness. Science is catching up with Scripture on this one. A recent study from Concordia University found that constant bitterness could make a person ill. Holding onto bitterness can affect metabolism, immune response, and organ function, and it can lead to physical disease, researchers say.

Your Self-Assessment

First, ask the Holy Spirit to spotlight any bitterness buried in your heart, remembering that roots can remain dormant for years. While in prayer, identify six people that have wounded you. It could be years ago or last month. Note their name, then give them a score, on a scale of 1 (doesn't hurt anymore) to 10 (hurts a great deal or caused lasting damage):

1) _____   _____

2) _____   _____

3) _____   _____

4) _____   _____

5) _____   _____

6) _____   _____

Scores of more than 2 are an indication that you need to be healed. Thinking about the people noted above, picture their faces one by one, and ask yourself the following questions:

☐ Does the sight of their face make my heart harden?

☐ When I think about what happened, do I feel agitated?

☐ Am I still angry or upset?

☐ Would I be happy if I heard that they had been abundantly blessed?

If you answered yes to one of the first three questions or no to the final question, please ask the Lord to do a deep work in your heart as you read. And please pray now for the Holy Spirit to highlight the issues He wants to tackle.

Who Is Responsible?

It is easy to discount particular Scriptures in certain seasons. Verses that seem relevant during the usual ups and downs of life can appear invalid during devastating situations. But Isaiah 40:8 is clear, "The grass withers, the flower fades, but the word of our God stands forever." We need to hold to the truth of God's Word through even the fiercest of storms.

Proverbs 4:23 (AMP) says, "Keep and guard your heart with all vigilance and above all that you guard..." This verse explains a vital truth. Each one of us is responsible for taking care of our own souls. When you have been wronged, it can feel right to hold someone else to account for your pain. Yes, they may have hurt you badly. However, Scripture asks you to accept responsibility for the condition of your heart. Let's look at the same verse in the New Living Translation: "Guard your heart above all else, for it determines the course of your life." (Proverbs 4:23 NLT) A terrible tragedy may have broken your precious heart. But please know that the traumas of the past do not have the power to decide your destiny. Your heart determines how your life turns out. You can pursue healing in every situation and come through even the cruelest of circumstances. You can embrace a bright future even after a dark past. Our hero Joseph is living proof that this is God's way.

Please ask the Lord to reveal anything in your heart that is holding you back. Proverbs 20:27 says, "The spirit of a man is the lamp of the Lord, searching all the inner depths of his heart." Your heart is deep. That's why even the Lord needs to search to find what's hiding inside. I can't tell you how many times our Heavenly Father has revealed deep wounds that I didn't know were holding me back. Allow the Lord to shine His light into your soul, not just for your sake, but also to ensure that you do not hurt those you love. Because bitterness has a bad reputation, it is easy to assume that we are immune. I encourage you to join me in seeking a spiritual deep clean. Let's ask the Lord to uncover any anger or resentment hiding inside. He will reveal the issue, but He will do much more. Your Heavenly Father will go to the pain that caused the problem in the first place. He will heal your heart so that you can enjoy your life. Let's pray before we go any further.

Heavenly Father,

I open my heart to You. I ask You to shine Your light into the depths of my soul and reveal any bitterness hiding inside. I don't want any upset or anger to repel Your favor. I don't want to contaminate others as a result of my own inner issues. I don't want to get stuck in the pain of the past. I choose today to accept responsibility for my heart, but I cannot fix myself, I need You, Lord. Please reveal buried pain in my heart, please cleanse me deep down so that my heart is a pleasant dwelling place for Your Spirit.

In Jesus' name I pray,

Amen.

The Pain Of Rejection

The sons of Jacob, whose stories are told in the Book of Genesis, were used powerfully in their generation and their offspring were mighty on the earth. Yet the Bible tells us that these men ended up hating their brother Joseph. The blatant favoritism that their father showed to their younger brother wounded these men. They watched while their father lavished his love on the dreamer. It made them feel rejected. When one sibling is singled out and celebrated, it can be awful for the others. Maybe you have been hurt that way. You could have a brother or sister who was the apple of your parent's eye. You may have longed to be loved the way that your father or mother adored them. The ache of rejection can be overwhelming.

Joseph's brothers were hurt, but they didn't know how to deal with their pain. Let me pause here. It is God's desire to heal you every time you are hurt. He does not want you to endure the agony of rejection; He longs for you to come into His presence and pour out your pain in prayer. That's what the Lord wanted for the sons of Jacob, too. The day that their dad gave Joseph a special gift was too much for them to handle. The sense of injustice was horrible. It wasn't fair that one son was loved so much. The wounds festered and produced hate. Genesis 37:3-4 (NLT) says, "Jacob loved Joseph more than any of his other children because Joseph had been born to him in his old age. So, one day Jacob had a special gift made for Joseph – a beautiful robe. But his brothers hated Joseph because their father loved him more than the rest of them..."

One of the Greek words for bitterness is 'pikria', which means bitter hatred. When bitterness takes root, hatred gets buried. The fruits of bitterness and hatred overlap to such an extent that understanding one will help us to grasp the other.

Spreads Like Cancer

Bitter hatred takes root when pain and anger fuse in the heart of a man. It festers and then it contaminates others. Let's look again at Hebrews 12:15 (NIV): "See to it that… no bitter root grows up to cause trouble and defile many." One of the hallmarks of bitterness is that it influences others. I suspect that hatred spread among the brothers of Joseph as a result of *one* of Joseph's brothers becoming bitter. Of course, his siblings will have all felt hurt, but hatred is not inevitable when you are wounded.

Psalms 33:15 says, "He fashions their hearts individually…" Your heart is uniquely designed by your Heavenly Father. No other heart is quite like yours. In the same way, each of Joseph's brothers was unique. Some of those young men will probably have been particularly tender, others may have been more tough. It would be almost impossible to imagine eleven young men all becoming enraged as a result of favoritism. It is far more likely that one or two might have been oblivious; a couple would probably have been sad but certainly not angry. It was probably just one who was eaten up by the sense of injustice which will have grown as he rehearsed the wrongs of favoritism. I would imagine that he shared his anger with the others which, as the Bible says, will have influenced all their opinions. Soon enough, they all wanted to destroy Joseph's dreams. This collective anger drove Joseph's brothers to beat him, strip him, and sell him into slavery. Hatred caused these good men to do terrible things.

I Can't Let Go

Jane spent years trying to forgive her sister Diane. She came to God in prayer time after time, but she was still riddled with resentment. Jane would visit her family with the best of intentions. Then she would become irritated and even disgusted by Diane's behavior. Jane wanted to forgive because she desired to please God, but it seemed like an impossibility. From a very young age, Diane humiliated Jane in front of family and friends. Things grew worse as Jane reached her teenage years. The ridicule now took place in front of peers in school. Her parents never protected her from the onslaught of cruelty which dominated both her home and school life. As a young adult, the big obstacle in Jane's life was her relationship with her sister.

After repeatedly trying and failing to forgive, Jane attended one of our events. It was there that she discovered that her real issue was hatred. Animosity and anger had entered her heart when she was a child. As I led her in prayer to lay down her hatred, she cried bitter tears, eventually letting go of all hostility. Jane exchanged her hate for God's wonderful love, which soon filled her heart. She then forgave with supernatural ease. For the first few months afterwards, Jane regularly asked the Lord to refill her with His love, but she never contended again with unforgiveness.

Leviticus 19:17-18 (NLT) says, "Do not nurse hatred in your heart for any of your relatives." When you have been mistreated by family, anger can take root. After all, we expect our nearest and dearest to love and protect us. When relationships break down, it can feel like a cruel betrayal. That's when animosity can start growing inside. But holding hatred against someone is like helping them to torture you. They probably sleep well at night while you are eaten up on the inside.

The Problem With Animosity

Although hating someone who has treated you terribly is understandable, it is never helpful. If we harbor hatred, it will harm us. It will also prevent us from moving on with our lives. 1 John 2:11 says, "He who hates his brother is in darkness and walks in darkness, and does not know where he is going, because the darkness has blinded his eyes." I don't know about you, but I want to find out God's will for my life. I want to see what God is doing in the world and what He wants to do in me. While we hate, it's as though we're walking around wearing a blindfold. Hate switches off God's light in our lives. Bitterness and hate are twins.

When it comes to our parents, the Bible goes further. A passage in Leviticus 20 shows us how seriously God views hate. There is a register of sins that God thinks are so serious that they deserve death (you must remember that this is the Old Testament, before Jesus shed His blood which is powerful enough to cleanse any sin). Included in this inventory are incest and bestiality, but at the top of the list of wrongs requiring death is cursing your father or mother (verse 9).

Cursing is dishonoring or discrediting your father or mother with your words. If you hate one of your parents, you may unwittingly find yourself cursing them. If you have been abused or abandoned by your father or mother, Satan may try to bury hate deep in your heart. The devil wants to bar you from the promises that are available to those who honor their parents. The Bible makes two wonderful pledges for those who show heartfelt respect for their parents: "Honor your father and your mother that your days may be long and that it may be well with you." Exodus 20:12.

The problem is that if I don't honor my parents, the enemy will have legal grounds to shorten my days and to block my prosperity. It's not enough for the enemy that you were wounded. He wants to make your life a mess and he would love to end it prematurely. That's why he resists the healing process so much. He knows better than anyone that when God heals your heart and you reject hatred and bitterness, you are on the road to restoration and happiness. Fruitfulness and blessing await you.

Tell Tale Signs

It's easy to think, "I'm just hurt and need healing." But great people can become bitter when they are wounded. It is better to face the truth and get delivered than remain in denial because it is difficult to swallow. The truth sets you free. We know the symptoms of common illnesses. As a result, doctors can diagnose what is wrong and prescribe the correct medicine. In the same way, the Bible tells us the symptoms of bitterness so that we can recognize the problem and apply the right remedy. As you read this list of symptoms, ask the Holy Spirit to expose any deep-rooted anger which the enemy has tried to hide in your heart. You may recognize just one of these symptoms, or you could see several at work in your life.

1. You're Stuck

Bitterness causes you to get stuck. Maybe you can't get past an unjust event, perhaps you struggle to move on after a brutal betrayal. Hebrews 12:15b says: "...Watch out that no poisonous root of bitterness grows up to trouble you, corrupting many." This Scripture explains that bitterness is a root. Roots grow deep into the ground and keep a tree or plant from moving. If you are bound up with bitterness, you will struggle to move forward. You may find yourself constantly thinking back to the pain of a difficult season. You may struggle to get past what happened. Any time you find yourself stuck, it is worth asking yourself if you are bitter.

2. Retelling Your Story

One man who suffered unimaginably is Job. He became bitter as a result of so much pain and injustice. I cannot imagine such grief and heartbreak. In one terrible accident, he lost all of his children. Not only that, his businesses collapsed and he became sick. In Job 10:1, he said: "...I give free course to my complaint, I will speak in the bitterness of my soul." When you are bitter, it affects your conversations. Firstly, it impacts what you say to yourself. When you have a bitter root, you can find yourself rehearsing what happened and what you wish you had said. All sorts of sights and circumstances cause you to think about the injustice. Each time you remember, old emotion is stirred. It makes your pain even harder to bear.

It also influences your conversations with others. You regularly talk about what happened. Matthew 12:34b (NIV) says, "...the mouth speaks what the heart is full of." When you are bitter, you will often retell your story. You probably miss details of any of your shortcomings and focus on the wrongs you suffered. You need others to know how much you went through and you want them to share your indignance. I have been there many times; it eats you up inside.

The Hebrew word for hate is 'satam' and it means to 'cherish animosity'. In other words, it suggests that there is almost enjoyment in loathing. Do you find it gratifying talking about how someone wronged you? Do you feel compelled to go back over what was said and done? Do you feel satisfied when someone else agrees with your point of view? The enemy makes sure that bitterness tastes sweet to the flesh.

3. You Set The Record Straight

If someone speaks well about someone who wronged you, you feel the need to set the record straight. It feels right to complain about their mistakes and to discuss their shortcomings. After all, they hurt you. If others respect them, you recall behavior that contradicts that admiration. Genesis 37:4 says, "When his brothers saw that their father loved him more... they hated him and could not speak a kind word to him." When you are bitter, antagonism and criticism are on your lips. Good words only come out through gritted teeth.

Maybe you want to do the right thing. You plan to be gracious and considerate, but you end up being harsh. You are left feeling disappointed, guilty, and frustrated. Bitter anger always finds its way out of our mouths. That's how is contaminates others. Remember Job 10:1 says, ...I will give free course to my complaint, I will speak in the bitterness of my soul." When hatred is hidden in our hearts, it will show up on our lips. Proverbs 6:16-19 describes seven attitudes the Lord abhors. The final heart issue mentioned is in Proverbs 6:19b: "...one who sows discord among brethren." God hates it when we say or do things that could bring division among God's people. When we are free from this issue, we enjoy new peace and freedom.

4. You Still Feel Wronged

When you are fully free from the pain of injustice, you no longer *feel* wronged. Of course, you still suffered the injustice, but hardness of heart is replaced by tenderness. In contrast, when bitterness is buried inside, you still feel agitated when you think about what happened. You may have resigned yourself to your new reality, but that is very different from being at peace with the past. Bitterness expects sympathy and remains focused on what went wrong. You become tethered to the event. It is draining.

Proverbs 10:12a says, "Hatred stirs up strife..." Strife is conflict, discord, and antagonism. When you are bitter, you find it hard to resist stirring up arguments with those you oppose. You seldom, if ever, agree with their point of view or support their efforts. You feel prickly and hostile when you see their face or hear their name. Proverbs 10:12 in the Passion Translation says, "Hatred keeps old quarrels alive..." This is an indicator that bitterness is hidden inside.

5. You Spy On The Ones Who Wronged You

Social media makes it tempting to 'spy' on people who have hurt you. You may visit their page, check their stories, or ask others for updates. You secretly gloat when things don't go well for them. You might give the impression that you're sad, but actually you feel a sense of satisfaction. On the other hand, if that person is doing well, you try to undermine their achievements. It does not seem right for them to experience success because of the things that they have done which hurt you.

Even after prayer, you may struggle to shift anger. Leviticus 19:17-18 indicates the relationship between bitterness and vengeance: "You shall not hate your brother in your heart... you shall not seek vengeance nor bear any grudge but you shall love your neighbor as yourself." Put simply, vengeance is wanting the person who hurt you to pay in some way. That might be in failed relationships, closed doors, ministry hiccups, or job losses.

6. You Want Them To Pay

Spite is a desire to frustrate, harm, or humiliate another person. Spite wants to hurt the people who wounded you. Maybe you don't want to cause pain yourself, but you want them to feel bad. This sounds like the Jewish people at the time of Jesus. John 18:31 says, "Then Pilate said to them, 'You take Him and judge Him according to your law. ' Therefore the Jews said to him, 'It is not lawful for us to put anyone to death.'" The Israelites wanted Jesus to be killed while complying with their religious rules, so they asked someone else to do their dirty work.

Do you want the people who have hurt you to have difficulties? Do you smile inside when they fall flat on their face and think to yourself, "You only got what was coming to you!" Proverbs 24:17-18 (AMP) says, "Rejoice not when your enemy falls, and let not your heart be glad when he stumbles or is overthrown, lest the Lord see it and it be evil in His eyes and displease Him, and He turn away His wrath from him [to expend it upon you, the worse offender]."

The Way Forward

All of the symptoms of bitterness are exhausting. Negative attitudes and habits are heavy and draining. In contrast, positive emotions such as love, mercy, and joy are light and energizing. Uprooting bitterness sets you free to fulfill your destiny, but it also enhances your quality of life. You will feel lighter, happier, and healthier once you have kicked this enemy out of your life. We are going to go look at some steps to help you on your journey to liberty.

1. The Road To Restoration

Bitterness almost always begins with a deep and painful wound. In order to be free, you need to be healed in the depths of your heart. Psalms 147:3 (TPT) says, "He heals the wounds of every shattered heart." There is no ache or agony that God cannot heal when we surrender every source of sadness in His presence. How do you do that? Well, pain is bound up with words. You were designed by the Lord with a divine connection between your heart and your mouth. When you express the deep issues of your heart to your Heavenly Father, you begin to release buried hurts. Matthew 12:34b says, "...out of the abundance of the heart the mouth speaks." As you share your pain in prayer, our God is able to reach into your soul and take your pain away.

Restoration can seem out of reach when you avoid looking at the *real* reason you felt so hurt. Sometimes the truth is painful. It can be easier to avoid what wounded you the most. When you face your truth, you can begin your journey to healing. If you don't know what hurt you the most, ask the Lord to show you. Psalms

44:21 (AMP) says, "Would not God discover this? For He knows the secrets of the heart." Even when you don't know the real reasons you feel so wronged, God knows. Ask Him to shine His light into your heart and show you where to start.

An Avalanche Of Pain

The evening after my spiritual mom died, I received a voice note from my son sharing his first ever sermon. I was blown away as I listened to my son share the word of God with such sensitivity. The anointing on his message was precious. As he summed up, I went to get myself a cup of coffee when suddenly an intense ball of pain surfaced. Falling to my knees, I cried out to the Lord, "I don't want to tell You about Benjy's message, I want to tell my spiritual mom!"

My spiritual mother prayed daily for my children and loved them dearly. It was my habit to share their milestones with her. The words that left my mouth may sound disrespectful, but they were my truth, and they released an avalanche of pain. I wept from the depths of my heart for about 20 minutes until my eyes dried and my heart calmed. When I woke up the following morning, I knew I was on my way to restoration. If I had bottled that pain because it seemed inappropriate, I believe I would have drawn out my healing journey.

What has hurt you the most? Please face the issues that have caused you pain or shame. Proverbs 23:23a says, "Buy the truth, and do not sell it..." This verse implies that truth comes at a cost. It may be hard to acknowledge what hurt but speaking the truth in prayer releases trapped pain. Lamentations 2:19 tells us what to do: "Arise, cry out in the night... Pour out your heart like water before the face of the Lord." Remember, there is a connection between your heart and your mouth, that's the way the Lord made you (see Luke 6:45). When you tell your Heavenly Father what you went through and how it made you feel, He will heal your heart. Usually, as you share what broke you, tears will flow.

Tears are a God-given mechanism to release pain. Just as urinating releases toxins from your body, crying releases anguish from your soul. However, there is one form of weeping that will not heal your wounds. Lamentations 1:2 says, "She weeps bitterly in the night, Her tears are on her cheeks... She has none to comfort her." Bitter tears are cried from anger and frustration. You can cry that way day after day without experiencing healing. The tears that bring restoration are born from a heart of surrender. As you weep, be sure to let go of your sadness and give your pain to the Lord. Those tears will lead to freedom.

When The Truth Is Uncomfortable

King Saul ended up bound by bitterness, but it didn't have to be that way. Let's look at part of his story. Saul was insecure. When Prophet Samuel told Saul that God had chosen him to be king, he doubted himself. Saul hid at his coronation and relied on people's praises to build his confidence. As king, Saul took a young warrior David under his wing. David loved the king and was loyal, almost to a fault. However, Saul became bitter toward David...

1 Samuel 18:7-8 tells the story: "So the women sang as they danced, and said: 'Saul has slain his thousands, and David his ten thousands.' Then Saul was very angry, and the saying displeased him; and he said, 'They have ascribed to David ten thousands, and to me they have ascribed only thousands. Now what more can he have but the kingdom?'" Saul told himself that the young warrior wanted to steal his throne, but this was obviously not Saul's real concern. The king felt inadequate when the people celebrated David. He did not like someone else being in the limelight. Saul could not stand hearing these women compare him with his spiritual son. It made him feel small.

If the king had gone into his secret place and told the Lord how the ladies' song made him feel, I'm certain that God would have healed his heart. If he had faced his truth, it could have led to his restoration. Instead, Saul became bitter and was soon determined to destroy David. Of course, the bitterness did not destroy David; it poisoned King Saul. Maybe you have been treated in ways that made you feel like a failure. Perhaps, like Saul, you have been publicly humiliated. Please don't turn away from the truth, even if it is uncomfortable. Talk to the Lord and ask Him to heal your precious heart.

Could You Be Angry With God?

Tragedy made Naomi (whose story is told in the book of Ruth) feel wronged by God. She believed that the Lord was against her. When Naomi returned home to Bethlehem, the people were excited to see her again after more than a decade. She silenced their joy in Ruth 1:20-21 with these words: "Do not call me Naomi; call me Mara, for the Almighty has dealt very bitterly with me. I went out full, and the Lord has brought me home again empty. Why do you call me Naomi, since the Lord has testified against me, and the Almighty has afflicted me?"

Naomi means pleasant whereas Mara means bitter. This grief-stricken woman was bitter because she thought that God was against her. It's important to note that Naomi was mistaken; it was not the Lord who caused her pain. When her late husband led his family to Moab, he probably led them out of the will of God. The center of God's will is always the safest place on earth, even if that means remaining in a nation that is suffering a famine. Naomi was mistaken about the identity of the perpetrator of her sorrow, but thankfully, she was in touch with the anguish of her soul and shared her disappointment.

If you feel let down by the Lord, please don't imagine that your relationship with Him is unaffected by your suffering. God is the God of truth, and He knows your struggles. Psalms 139:2 (TPT) says, "You perceive every movement of my heart and soul, and you understand my every thought before it even enters my mind."

In fact, Psalm 51:6 tells us that He desires the truth. The "man after God's own heart" (see 1 Samuel 13:14) shared every anguish with the Lord in prayer. He told God when he felt let down. David became a wonderful example of how to pour out our hearts before the Lord.

Tell your Heavenly Father how you feel and release every sense of injustice in His presence. Please don't hold onto your hurts, it will only hold you back in life. Surrender your distress. It is possible to be honest without being dishonorable. Listen to King David's prayer in Psalms 13:1-3 (NLT): "O Lord, how long will you forget me? Forever? How long will you look the other way? How long must I struggle with anguish in my soul, with sorrow in my heart every day? How long will my enemy have the upper hand? Turn and answer me, O Lord my God! Restore the sparkle to my eyes, or I will die." Without hardening his heart, David poured out his pain in prayer, and God healed his soul.

2. Changing Your Conversations

"Jo, don't tell that story again," the Lord was clear. I had shared the pain of a particular season one time too many and it had to stop. Explaining what happened to those who can help is one thing. But repeating the details of painful experiences again and again will keep you stuck in victimhood. If you want to be free from the burden of bitterness, it is time to refrain from telling people your story. You need to share your pain in prayer, but there will come a time when you'll need to stop telling others.

If you were monitoring the people who hurt you, it is also important to stop spying. It only fuels the wrong feelings. Make a decision to close that door and leave the past behind you. Don't visit that social media page again. Stop asking mutual friends what the wrongdoer is up to. Your future lies ahead of you. You can't get there by dwelling on the people and the pain of the past. Philippians 3:13 says, "...one thing I do, forgetting those things which are behind and reaching forward to those things which are ahead." Leaving the past behind will enable you to embrace a brighter future.

3. Kick Out Animosity

We were made in the image of God, and God is love. Love is what we do best because we were designed to love and not to despise. If you have been holding hatred in your heart, it is time to ask the Lord to take it away. If you realize that you hate – or have hated – your father or mother, now is the chance to deal with it and to shut the door on the devil. Perhaps it's not your parents. Maybe you recognize that you have animosity in your heart towards someone who has hurt you or a person you once trusted. God showed me a wonderful way of breaking hate's power. Bring the hate to the Lord as an offering. Ask Him to receive the hate in your heart as an act of surrender to His ways and His love. Picture yourself bringing this hatred to the cross of Jesus and laying it down as a sacrifice. At the cross, Christ broke the power of hate by His love.

Then ask Him to cleanse your heart. Repent of any negative words spoken and anything done to repay evil for evil. Ask Him to forgive you for curses spoken, unkind words shared, bad attitudes, evil wishes, and grudges. Ask Him to cleanse you of every remnant of hate – He is able! In exchange for hate, ask God to pour His unconditional love into your life. Proverbs 10:12 (TPT) says, "Hatred keeps old quarrels alive, but love draws a veil over every insult and finds a way to make sin disappear." Ask the Lord to fill your heart with His love for those you once hated. Ask for more than enough love for every day. Once you have dealt with hate, it will be so much easier to forgive.

4. The Power Of Forgiveness

Our first child died before her second birthday after contracting a bacterial infection. A simple injection of antibiotics on arrival at hospital would have saved Naomi's life. If the doctor who was charged with caring for our little girl had done her job, our daughter would be with us today. Instead, Naomi lay on a hospital bed getting weaker while the medics did nothing. The doctor in charge insisted on waiting for a urine sample before giving our sweetheart antibiotics. As hours passed, I grew more desperate until I took matters into my own hands. I pressed upon my little girl's tummy, holding a bowl underneath. I managed to squeeze out a trickle of urine, I handed it to the doctor who then administered antibiotics. But it was too late. The infection had spread through Naomi's tiny frame, causing multiple organ failure. She passed away a few hours later.

Shortly after her death, my husband and I knelt down before the Lord with tears running down our cheeks and forgave the medic who was involved in our little girl's death. We asked God to bless her life and family. We worked with senior practitioners to ensure new procedures were introduced at the hospital so that no other child would suffer unnecessarily. However, we chose to let go of the terrible injustice of Naomi's death. Any time we thought of that doctor, we asked God to be with her and to help her. I believe our heartfelt forgiveness released the healing love of God into our shattered lives. Every time I cried out to Him, He tended my brokenness, and bit by bit, He put my heart back together. Today, I have no sadness over our daughter's untimely departure. I am deeply grateful that the Lord has restored us and that we will pick up as parents where we left off when we are reunited with Naomi in heaven.

The Way To Freedom

Maybe a trusted friend betrayed you. Perhaps your spouse cheated on you. A colleague might have taken the credit for your idea. Did your family abandon you when you needed them most? When someone has wronged you, it can be hard to let it go. But no matter what has been done to you, forgiveness is the way to your freedom. When we hold something against someone, we are inadvertently holding onto that person. Because we won't let go of what they did, we cannot let go of them either. Unforgiveness keeps us bound to the events and people of the past. Job 5:2 (NLT) says, "Resentment destroys the fool..."

After 37 years of marriage, Angela went through a devastating divorce. Her husband had beaten her, cheated on her, and withheld money that was rightfully hers. She felt humiliated, heartbroken, and was at the point of breakdown. Angela became consumed with bitterness and hate. Pastors, friends, and family tried to persuade her, but she found it impossible to forgive. She wanted revenge and longed for something terrible to happen to her ex-husband.

Someone gave Angela my book *Lifting the Mask*, and hope began to grow in her heart. When she heard how God helped us to forgive the doctor on duty when our daughter died, she began to believe that the Holy Spirit could help her, too. Angela allowed the love of the Lord to flood into her heart and wash away years of bitterness. She forgave her husband and relinquished her right to retaliation. For the first time in years, Angela experienced peace and genuine joy. Several months later, she bumped into her ex-husband at a family function. Walking towards him, she reached out her hand and greeted him warmly. The look of shock on his face was priceless. Angela was free.

Forgiving Daily

For ten years King Saul, the man David once called 'Father' hunted him down, determined to kill him. The young man lived rough, hiding in caves and forests while Saul sent soldiers to execute him. Day in, day out, David lived in fear of his life. Saul was consumed by hate for the young man simply because he had won the hearts of the people. Maybe you can relate to this; you are trapped in a situation which causes ongoing pain. Remember that we are instructed to forgive, whereas trust is a choice. Forgiveness is free, whereas trust us earned.

On two occasions, David had the chance to kill the king, but he refused to touch the Lord's anointed. Each time the opportunity presented itself, it was at a point when Saul himself sought to murder David. Despite having every excuse to retaliate, David restrained himself and even spoke respectfully to Saul when he explained why he had spared the king's life. David lived a life of forgiveness. He let go of anger on a daily basis and kept a tender heart towards a man who made his life like a living hell. He even spoke of the King with love at his death. No wonder God called him a man after His heart. Within about a week of Saul's passing, David was crowned King of Judah. I believe his forgiving heart secured his destiny.

Can you relate to David? Perhaps you have been hurt again and again by family or friends. Your pain might not be in the past; it could be a daily battle. Like David, if you keep forgiving, you will pave the way to fulfill your purpose. Remember, forgiveness is essential whereas trust is a choice. Forgiveness uproots bitterness and releases you from the pain of the past. Do not listen to the devil's lies anymore. The only person who suffers if you do not forgive is you.

Debt Cancellation

The parable in Matthew 18:23-35 tells the story of a king who wanted to settle accounts with his servants. A man was brought to him who owed a huge debt, but he was unable to pay. The king had compassion and wrote off his debt. That very servant left the king's presence and forced a fellow servant to pay a tiny debt. He refused to show the compassion that he had received. When the king heard what the servant had done, he was furious and threw his servant into prison until he paid everything he owed.

When someone has wronged you, you feel like they owe you something. They have taken from you and must pay back. Forgiveness is writing off their debt because your debt has already been cancelled. It is releasing a person from what they owe. But here is the thing: when a person owes you money, the debt connects the two of you. When you cancel their debt, the link between your lives is broken. You can leave the past behind and embrace your future. Forgiveness releases *you* from captivity. As you let go of every wrong, bitterness will be uprooted. As you release all anger, God will fill your heart with His perfect peace. Ephesians 4:31-32 (NLT) says, "Get rid of all bitterness, rage, anger, harsh words, and slander, as well as all types of evil behavior. Instead, be kind to each other, tenderhearted, forgiving one another, just as God through Christ has forgiven you." We will pray together at the end of this chapter.

5. Seal Your Freedom

After you have forgiven those who have hurt you, there is a final step that will seal your freedom. Matthew 5:44 says, "But I say to you, love your enemies, bless those who curse you, do good to those who hate you, and pray for those who spitefully use you and persecute you." Jesus instructed you and me to bless those who curse and to pray for those who are spiteful. This is a powerful way of closing the door on bitterness.

Once you have released your anger in God's presence, it is time to bless. If the person in question is still alive, pray for them. Ask God to bless their family, their ministry, or their business. Ask Him to heal their heart and bring restoration to their lives. The act of blessing will bring a lightness to your heart, it will set you apart from the weight of anger. While Stephen was being stoned to death, "...he knelt down and cried out with a loud voice, 'Lord, do not charge them with this sin.'" (Acts 7:60) The Apostle did not want the people to pay for their sin against him; he asked the Lord to release them.

It would be my honor to lead you in prayer. We will deal with the various steps covered in this chapter. I encourage you to pray with me the whole way through. However, if any section is not relevant, jump to the next. Let's pray.

Heavenly Father,

I open my heart to You, Lord, and I ask You to do a new work in my life. I want to be free to fulfill my destiny, so I ask for Your help to uproot every trace of bitterness from my heart.

Bitter Words

Words have been spoken that cut me to the core. Those words pierced my heart and I find myself remembering them often. Today I bring those words to You. (*Now tell the Lord what was said, who said it, and how it made you feel. Share the impact that those words have had in your life. If there are several comments that have come to mind, deal with them one by one.*) I remove those fiery darts from my heart in Jesus' name. I ask You to heal me of the pain they caused. I forgive (insert their name) from my heart. I let go what was said.

Feeling Hurt By God

Father, I don't understand why You allowed me to suffer. I feel let down, I feel like You were not there when I needed You the most, and it hurts. But I realize that I was wrong. You are a good Father and You only ever have my best interests at heart. I release my anger. I let go of every sense of injustice because I know that You are just. I place my trust in You again, Lord. I thank You that You are for me, You have never been against me. You are a good Father and I am grateful for Your love. I love You and I ask You to heal my heart.

Healing

I was badly hurt, Lord. It was not fair and it was not right. (*Now tell the Lord exactly what happened and how it made you feel. Share your heart with God. Pour out your pain. Acknowledge the things that hurt you the most and explain to your Wonderful Counsellor why it was so painful.*) Heal my heart, Oh Lord, I pray. I surrender all my sadness and every sense of injustice. I lay it down before You. Take my pain away. I ask You to restore my soul.

Hatred And Bitterness

Lord, I realize that I have harbored hatred and bitterness in my heart. I don't want to hold this animosity anymore. So today, I bring this hatred to you as an offering. I give it to You; I don't want it anymore, it is Yours now, Lord. I release every ounce of anger and lay it down at Your altar. I ask that You would take it away from me now. Instead, I pray that You would fill me with Your wonderful love.

Forgiveness

I am so sorry, Lord, for holding onto anger and unforgiveness and I ask You to forgive me. I am so sorry for defiling other people with my bitterness. Forgive me, Lord, I pray. Today I choose to forgive those who hurt me because You always forgive me my trespasses. I choose to forgive so that I can be free from the burden of bitterness. I choose to forgive for the sake of my future. I forgive (*tell the Lord who you forgive and what you forgive them for. If you need to forgive several people, take your time. Forgive each one for each wrong done and for each hurt caused.*). I let go of the wrong you did. I release you, I let you go. I write off your debt, you don't owe me anything. I forgive you from my heart.

Seal Your Healing

If the one who hurt you is still alive, pray: Father, I ask You to bless (*insert their name*), I ask You to bless their health, their family, and their life. I ask You to heal their heart and help them to live the life that You have for them.

If the one who hurt you has passed away: Father, I bless the memory of (*insert their name*). From now on, I will not speak about wrong suffered. Father, I ask You to remove every trace of bitterness from my heart. Cleanse me from the inside out. Make me new and fill me afresh with Your precious Spirit.

In Jesus' name I pray,

Amen.

Chapter Four

THE DISEASE THAT DRAINS

As I was scrolling through social media one day, I saw an image of a woman enjoying success. I didn't know this lady very well, but instinctively I felt dissatisfied. My musings were subtle, but somewhere under the surface, I was thinking, "That's not fair. Why does she deserve this breakthrough?" As I continued looking at the post, my heart began to harden. I found myself questioning her motives and assuming that she was somewhat superficial. A series of critical assumptions hovered just beneath the surface. I was not really conscious of my thoughts until the Holy Spirit showed me my heart...

Jeremiah 17:9 (AMP) explains, "The heart is deceitful above all things, and it is exceedingly perverse and corrupt and severely, mortally sick! Who can know it [perceive, understand, be acquainted with his own heart and mind]?" I prided myself on having high levels of self-awareness. I even taught others how to know what is going on inside! And yet I had no idea that discontent was hidden in my heart. If you had asked me if I was prone to envy, I would have replied that I was aware of my many weaknesses, but that envy was not one of them. The Holy Spirit had a different perspective.

Why Do Unconscious Thoughts Matter?

God considers the motives and intents of our hearts to evaluate our readiness for promotion. Remember, when the Lord was searching for a man to replace King Saul, the Lord examined the state of His children's hearts. God overlooked a man that even Prophet Samuel assumed would be first choice, in favor of someone who had a heart void of selfish ambition and full of love. 1 Samuel 16:7 (NLT) says, "But the Lord said to Samuel, 'Don't judge by his appearance or height, for I have rejected him. The Lord doesn't see things the way you see them. People judge by outward appearance, but the Lord looks at the heart.'"

I had no idea that a destiny blocker had locked an important door to my God-given dreams. Not only that, the Lord revealed that this was not a 'one-off' response. He showed me that I often begrudged hearing that particular people were succeeding. Hardness of heart is a serious issue. The Lord kept an entire generation out of their Promised Land because of this issue. Jesus sternly corrected His disciples when their hearts were hard. This is not a small matter to the Lord. It is not just what is in your heart that counts, it is also your heart's condition.

For a long time, I had known that God had called me to minister through television. Before my first appearance on a TV show, my husband warned me how strange speaking to a camera feels. However, even my first interview on Christian TV felt natural. I looked at the camera and could visualize precious people in their homes. It felt personal. As I launched different books and was invited onto various shows, it became normal for producers to tell me that I was a natural. It was obvious that God had called me to minister through the media.

The Lord has many ways to prepare you for your destiny, and this is one: He gives you a taste of fulfillment ahead of time. God creates the opportunity for you to sample your high call. This sows desire in your heart which will give you the motivation to pursue God's plans. James 1:15 says, "...when desire has conceived, it gives birth..." Desire is a powerful force! It gets you up in the morning and keeps you going when you are tired.

It keeps a dream alive on the inside when there is no evidence of manifestation. Hunger propels you. It generates the motivation you need to persevere.

I tasted the joy of ministering through television. The desire to reach multitudes via the media grew on the inside of me and propelled me to keep believing for a breakthrough. Have you ever noticed that the focus of your heart shows up all around you? When you are pregnant, you spot expectant moms everywhere. When you are believing for a certain model of car, you see your dream vehicle at every junction. Well, I saw television opportunities everywhere I looked! But the majority were being enjoyed by other people, and I didn't like what I saw.

Perverting The Purpose Of Testimony

This is where the enemy seeks to skew our view. Acts 10:34b (NLT) says, "...I see very clearly that God shows no favoritism..." Jesus does not show partiality. What the Lord has done for your friend, He wants to do for you. Instead of seeing a brother's breakthrough as a reason to complain, God wants you and I to see the blessings enjoyed by others as a source of encouragement! What your Heavenly Father has done for one of His children, He will do again.

The purpose of a testimony is firstly to glorify the Lord. When a child of God testifies of His goodness, they are vocalizing their gratitude. The Bible tells us that God hears our thoughts as well as our words. Matthew 9:4 says, "But Jesus, knowing their thoughts, said, 'Why do you think evil in your hearts?'" Imagine how awful it must sound in heaven when a Christian resents hearing the heartfelt praises of their brother or sister? Testimony has another purpose. It is designed to stir hope in the hearts of the hearers. The story that the Lord wants to use to build your faith, Satan wants to use to stir envy.

What happens in your heart when you see your hopes and dreams pictured in someone else's story? Especially when you don't much like the one sharing their breakthrough? How do you feel when an *undeserving* sister is given the reward you were hoping for? (Undeserving is italicized because, of course, only God actually knows who deserves to be blessed.) How do you react when someone who has only just joined your organization gets promoted over you? What goes on inside when a co-worker gets recognized for your hard work? Do you harden? Do you feel short-changed or let down? Do you get irritated with the one who is celebrating? How do you react when a minister enjoys frequent vacations or if they move to a big house? Does it rub you up the wrong way? And if so, why? Deep down, what are you feeling?

When I realized that I had been harboring hardness in my heart, I apologized. My Heavenly Father has always been so faithful to me, my dissatisfaction was full of entitlement and ingratitude. I told the Lord how sorry I was for such an awful attitude. I asked Him to forgive me and to change me from the inside out. The Holy Spirit gave me some homework. I started to pray daily for anyone I once envied. I asked the Lord to shower them with His favor, I asked Him to open up exciting new doors and to grant them the desires of their hearts. I prayed for Him to do more for them than they had asked or imagined. It was not long before discontent turned to gladness and my hard heart became tender toward those servants of God.

The Roots Of Discontent

The definition of discontent is 'a craving for something that you do not have'. It is dissatisfaction. Discontent has self at the center, and when it turns into words, it becomes a complaint. Speaking of the children of Israel during their wilderness experience, 1 Corinthians 10:10 (MSG) says, "We must be careful not to stir up discontent; discontent destroyed them." They were dissatisfied during times of trial and moaned about their difficulties. This heart attitude kept them – and it can keep us – from possessing the promises of God. Ingratitude is one heart condition that feeds discontent. Another is envy. If witnessing a brother being blessed makes you feel shortchanged, that is envy. The definition of envy is 'a feeling of *discontent* when confronted by another's advantages, successes, or possessions'. Envy causes you to be upset when someone else is favored.

Desire is the unadulterated version of envy. The Greek word 'zēloō' is translated in 1 Corinthians 14:1 as desire: "Pursue love, and desire spiritual gifts…" When my eyes are on what God wants to do for me, desire is pure. We must keep our desires focused on God's promises and on His ability to provide. When desire focuses on the advantages that someone else is enjoying, it decays into envy. This is one way the enemy tries to defile people with great dreams. The same Greek word zēloō is used in Acts17:5 in its defiled form. The eyes of a few Jews were on the popularity and success that the Apostles were enjoying. They wanted what God had given someone else and so their desire had become corrupted. In this verse, the word is translated as envious. Acts 17:5a says, "But the Jews… becoming envious…" Envy is a destiny blocker that the devil uses to delay or even derail God's people. It is inseparable from discontent.

Let's look at ourselves for a moment. When times are tough, when you're browsing social media or observing life or the people around you, do you ever think thoughts like those that follow?

☐ He doesn't deserve that.

☐ This isn't fair, I've been waiting too long.

☐ Why did it happen for her?

☐ I've had enough of the way things are going.

☐ Not them again, I don't know why they keep getting celebrated.

☐ I'm fed up of waiting, why are there so many delays?

☐ They are always on vacation!

☐ Can't you drive any faster? You're too slow.

☐ I don't like what I'm hearing.

☐ That's not fair, it's my turn.

☐ I can't believe I've been standing in line this long!

☐ Why do they flaunt their blessings?

☐ I wish they would do what I want, just for once.

If you ever find yourself feeling shortchanged or disgruntled, God wants to do a wonderful work in your heart and life. Not only will this make the way for new destiny doors to open, it will also dramatically enhance the quality of your life.

A Subtle Door Opener To Discontent

The tragic story of Queen Vashti's fall from favor is told in the book of Esther. Married to King Xerxes, who reigned over a vast territory stretching from India in Asia to Ethiopia in Africa, Vashti lived with her husband in a magnificent palace. Early in the king's reign, he decided to throw an enormous party. This long, drawn-out feast was important to King Xerxes as he established his rule. Influential men across his empire were invited to the celebrations, where wine was flowing in abundance.

At the same time, Queen Vashti gathered the ladies, who enjoyed their own festivities. Esther 1:10-12 (NLT) explains what happened, "On the seventh day of the feast, when King Xerxes was in high spirits because of the wine, he told the seven eunuchs who attended him... to bring Queen Vashti to him with the royal crown on her head. He wanted the nobles and all the other men to gaze on her beauty, for she was a very beautiful woman. But when they conveyed the king's order to Queen Vashti, she refused to come. This made the king furious, and he burned with anger."

Vashti was enjoying the privileges that being a queen afforded her. Maybe she had started to take her influential position for granted. She was probably having a splendid time with the leading ladies. Perhaps Vashti was repulsed by the king's drunkenness, or she may have felt patronized by the summons: "Who does he think he is? I don't want to parade myself in front of dozens of intoxicated men!" We don't know her exact thoughts, but I believe that an all-too-common character trap resulted in her refusing the king. It is called entitlement, and it breeds discontent. Vashti failed to remember that everything she had was given to her by Xerxes. She had become so accustomed to her privileges that she forgot that she was called to serve. Let's look at two ingredients of this modern-day destiny destroyer.

It's My Right

Entitlement makes you believe that positive circumstances are your right. When all is well, you are satisfied, but if things don't go to plan, you're displeased. It stirs a sense of let-down inside and you feel shortchanged. Entitlement fuels feelings of dissatisfaction when you don't get what you want. Maybe you migrated to another nation and find yourself working a job well below your skill set. Your focus is on what you don't have, rather than on the joys of your new life. Perhaps you had high hopes for a special birthday celebration then felt let down by friends or family. Assumptions about what others would do to celebrate you left you feeling disappointed. You could have worked your whole life in a particular company only to have someone half your age promoted to be your boss. If such circumstances cause displeasure, it could be time to drive out this destiny derailing attitude.

The Bible never promises us an easy life. Jesus, our example, was born in a shed, laid in a trough, and faced terrible difficulties throughout His time on earth. Despite appalling treatment, He was always grateful to God. Philippians 2:5-8 (NLT) says, "You must have the same attitude that Christ Jesus had. Though he was God, he did not think of equality with God as something to cling to. Instead, he gave up his divine privileges; he took the humble position of a slave and was born as a human being. When he appeared in human form, he humbled himself in obedience to God…"

High Expectations

The second issue with entitlement is that it creates unreasonable expectations of others. When I am entitled, I expect certain conduct from the people around me. I may tell myself that I am only asking of others what I do myself, nevertheless, the underlying heart issue is entitlement. When they don't live up to my ideals, I get upset. What people do rarely feels enough. As a result, it causes displeasure. If you bring entitlement into your relationship with the Lord, you will believe that breakthrough is your right. You will feel entitled to the benefits of God, rather than grateful every time you receive from Him. You could be thankful for a while, but a restless anticipation for your next blessing quickly builds again. This can make you prone to disappointment when your dreams aren't realized or if you face delays. Entitlement drains your joy and saps your strength.

Certain cultures foster entitlement. They teach that because your parents raised you, when you grow up, you must look after them. If an aunty or uncle helped you during childhood, there is the sense that you owe them when you are an adult. God loves all His children unconditionally. He gave His best – without strings attached. It is the Lord's desire that we love our children, nieces, nephews – and our neighbors – the same way. We love sacrificially, seeking nothing in return. Of course, we need to communicate the importance of honor to those we nurture, but we need to teach those principles for their sakes alone.

What Causes Entitlement?

Queen Vashti felt entitled to respect. She did not want anyone to tell her how to behave. The queen refused the king who had given her all that she had, and she lost everything (See Esther 1:19). We never hear of her again. In Vashti's case, this dangerous heart issue was probably incubated by a wrong response to privilege and position. Every opportunity you enjoy, every platform you stand on, every promotion you receive, is a gift from God. The devil will try to use the very success that the Lord has given you to make you feel deserving of certain standards. We must remember what Philippians 2:3b says, "...in loneliness of mind, let each esteem others as better than himself." God gives you gifts so that you can serve others. Position enables you to help as many people as possible. Luke 12:48b explains, "For everyone to whom much is given, from him much will be required; and to whom much has been committed, of him they will ask the more." Put simply, this verse says that the more we have, the more we must serve.

Sometimes, suffering creates entitlement. After our daughter died, I felt I deserved special treatment. I thought bad attitudes should be excused. If I was rejoicing, I believed I should be awarded a medal. Tragedy made me think that I should be given extra respect. People 'owed' me their compassion all the time. Perhaps your past pain has made you feel that you deserve special concessions. Maybe terrible injustice has caused you to have high expectations of others. You could feel as though the world owes you because you have faced far too much difficulty. No matter where it comes from, entitlement is a trap, and it is rooted in self-importance. It also opens the door to other destiny blockers.

Entitlement is the devil's counterfeit of favor. When I am entitled, I expect to be treated with respect. When I am favored, my heart attitude attracts generosity and goodwill. Entitlement believes it deserves recognition, favor gratefully receives God's blessings. When we harbor this unpleasant heart issue, it actually blocks the blessings we believe we deserve because it is rooted in pride. James

4:6 (TPT) says, "...God resists you when you are proud but continually pours out grace when you are humble." Grace is favor, so any time we allow these attitudes to creep into our hearts, we are in danger of repelling God's favor.

Thankfully, dealing with this character trap is simple. Let's go back to our core verses: "You must have the same attitude that Christ Jesus had. Though he was God, he did not think of equality with God as something to cling to. Instead, he gave up his divine privileges; he took the humble position of a slave..." (Philippians 2:5-7 NLT). Entitlement will probably derail your destiny, but emptying yourself will propel you into your purpose. Lay down every sense of entitlement. Give up the idea that success is your right and let go of all false expectations. You will be casting off a very heavy burden! Then ask the Lord to clothe you with true humility.

The Symptoms Of Discontent

Psalm 106 describes the attitudes that prevented the Israelites from entering the Promised Land. One of their biggest issues was discontent. They complained when life was tough, forgetting the blessings that they had previously received. Psalms 106:25b (NLT) says, "...they grumbled in their tents..." Notice, they didn't complain publicly, but our God who sees hearts was listening to their whining behind closed doors. They also compared themselves with Moses and Aaron and criticized their leadership: "...they envied Moses in the camp, and Aaron the saint of the Lord..." (Psalms 106:16) And finally, they were never satisfied with what they had. When God provided mana, they got fed up of that; when He gave them quails, they soon tired of meat. They were never satisfied.

Let's look again at the story of Cain. Comparison which we covered in Chapter Two led to discontent. Genesis 4:3-7 (AMP) says: "And in the course of time Cain brought to the Lord an offering of the fruit of the ground. And Abel brought of the firstborn of his flock and of the fat portions. And the Lord had respect and regard for Abel and for his offering, but for Cain and his offering He had no respect or regard. So, Cain was exceedingly angry and indignant, and he looked sad and depressed. And the Lord said to Cain, 'Why are you angry? And why do you look sad and depressed and dejected? If you do well, will you not be accepted? And if you do not do well, sin crouches at your door; its desire is for you, but you must master it.'"

In this short passage, Cain displayed some of the symptoms that surface when discontent is lurking beneath the surface. Before we go any further, let's ask for the help of the Spirit of Truth. Remember, the devil wants to disguise these destiny blockers so that they can remain unrestrained in your heart. In contrast, it is the desire of your Heavenly Father to expose anything that is holding you back. He longs to deal with hidden issues so that you can be free to succeed in every area of your life. Let's pray.

Heavenly Father,

I don't want to harbor any attitudes that grieve Your Spirit. I long to be free so that I can fulfill my destiny and bring glory to Jesus. Lord, I ask You to shine Your light into the depths of my soul as I read. Reveal any thoughts, habits, or behaviors that are rooted in envy or discontent. Cleanse me, Oh Lord, of all discontent and transform me into the image of Your Son.

In Jesus' name I pray,

Amen.

Just before we dive into some of the symptoms of discontent, I want to share some good news. Once you identify this heart issue, it is actually quite easy to kick out. Don't allow yourself to feel condemned as you read. Instead, see this as an opportunity to demolish one of the devil's plans to hold you back. We are advancing by exposing the work of the enemy. Not only that, when you rid yourself of this destiny blocker, you will enjoy a more abundant life.

1. Feeling Discouraged

According to the Bible, Cain looked "...sad, depressed and dejected..." (Genesis 4:5 AMP) He was feeling 'down in the dumps' and discouraged. This is a subtle symptom of discontent. When you feel discouraged, you may assume that difficult circumstances, or even the devil, are getting you down. However, this destiny blocker has the same effect. It causes you to focus on what's wrong and not on what's right. Forlorn thoughts cause sadness and make you feel disheartened. Cain interpreted his situation through a discontented viewpoint.

The way to work out what is behind your feelings is to trace back to the moment your sadness started. If melancholy was triggered by bad news, a disappointment, or a hurtful situation, then ask the Lord to heal you deep down. Pour out your pain in prayer. However, if it was prompted by slow progress or the news of an acquaintance being promoted, this is discontent. We are going to discover how to uproot this destiny blocker so that you can thrive.

2. Getting Annoyed

This heart issue makes you feel shortchanged or wronged; it seems as though life is unfair. Annoyance builds inside and fuels feelings of injustice. The more you dwell on your discontent, the less you are able to see the goodness of God or people. Cain was "... exceedingly angry and indignant..." (Genesis 4:5 AMP) You could get irritated with folk who are enjoying the life that you desire. You may resent those around you being promoted or celebrated. Psalms 68:16 says, "Why do you fume with envy..." Envy causes a stirring of negativity inside.

Cain was cross that his brother had succeeded where he failed. Indignance is displeasure at something that *feels* unjust. Notice Cain felt it was unjust, but he was wrong in this regard. We need to learn to discern between factual and fictional feelings. Just because I feel something, that does not necessarily mean that it is legitimate. Proverbs 25:28 (AMP) says, "He who has no rule over his own spirit is like a city that is broken down and without walls." We need to manage our emotions and ignore those reactions that are not based on truth. By quickly shutting down a fleeting thought, you can save yourself a great deal of unnecessary anguish.

To fulfill your purpose, you need to be able to take feedback. It is vital that you can be told where your strengths lie and what you need to work on to improve. If you struggle when people point out your shortcomings, my course Dreamstealers Online (see JoNaughton.com), will help you to be healed and transformed. Cain became angry because he did not like being told he was wrong. He could not handle being 'overshadowed' by his twin brother.

3. Finding Fault

Discontent triggers complaint. Often that comes in the form of harping back to the 'good ole days'. If you feel as though your best seasons are behind you, or that the past was almost perfect, your perspective needs to change for the sake of your future. We are drawn towards the focus of our thoughts. If you are constantly looking backwards, you will get stuck. Ecclesiastes 7:10 highlights the dangers of this: "...'Why were the former days better than these?' For you do not inquire wisely concerning this." It is not wise to look back with wonder unless that is to give God glory.

When I saw acquaintances enjoying the success I craved, I instinctively looked for faults. I hardly knew the women that I envied, yet I made negative assumptions about their characters.

Jeremiah 17:9 (MSG) says, "The heart is hopelessly dark and deceitful, a puzzle that no-one can figure out." Finding fault in those who are succeeding is an unhealthy defense mechanism. It is a means of avoiding facing what you really feel. Sadly, I believe my reactions were probably rooted in pride.

Sometimes fault-finding is motivated by insecurity. If you feel inferior, then the achievements of others may make you feel even worse. Criticizing those who are succeeding excuses your failure. Of course, slow progress is *not* failure, but that's what an insecure heart thinks. If you struggle with insecurity, Dreamstealers Online will lead you to healing and freedom. But even while you're on your healing journey, you can destroy this destiny blocker.

The Jews around at the time of the early church behaved in similar ways. Scripture tells us that they disliked the Apostles' popularity. Large numbers of people were attending Paul's meetings, so the Jews criticized the Apostle. Acts 13:45 says, "But when the Jews saw the multitudes, they were filled with envy; and contradicting and blaspheming, they opposed the things spoken by Paul." When you struggle with discontent, you may be prone to finding fault in the people who magnify your sense of dissatisfaction.

4. Being Unkind

Cain probably loved his brother and yet he ended up murdering his own flesh and blood. You may not have committed a crime, but discontent and envy bring the worst out of us all. God chose the sons of Jacob to be the founding leaders of the nation of Israel. Each one of them had a great call on their lives. Despite being raised in a God-fearing home, these men of destiny became cruel when they allowed dissatisfaction and envy to incubate in their hearts. Acts 7:9 says, "And the patriarchs, becoming envious, sold Joseph into Egypt..."

There are several examples in Scripture of envy producing cruelty. When David rose to popularity, jealousy caused King Saul to send armies to kill the young man he once loved like a son. The Apostles suffered much cruelty as a result of envy. Acts 17:5 says, "But the Jews who were not persuaded, becoming envious, took some of the evil men from the marketplace, and gathering a mob, set all the city in an uproar and attacked the house of Jason, and sought to bring them out to the people."

When we take our eyes off the goodness of God and dwell on our disappointments, we can end up feeling let down by life. That can cause us to implode and resent the blessings that others are enjoying. When that happens, even good people can behave in ways that are unkind or cruel. It's time to get this enemy out of our lives.

The Unwanted Results Of Discontent

Although we do not live under the Old Covenant, the Old Testament gives us important insights into the heart of God: "Soon the people began to complain about their hardship, and the Lord heard everything they said. Then the Lord's anger blazed against them, and he sent a fire to rage among them, and he destroyed some of the people in the outskirts of the camp." (Numbers 11:1 NLT) The Israelites were not grumbling on the mountaintop. That would be very ungrateful. They were complaining about their hardships en route to their destiny. It cannot have been easy to walk through the wilderness in soaring temperatures without a permanent resting place. Young families, pregnant ladies, nursing mothers, and very old people. They all had to walk, day after day. If you are anything like me, you probably enjoy a variety of food. They had to eat the same meals every day for years! Despite the difficulty of their circumstances, God saw their discontent as an appalling display of ingratitude.

Thank God for the cross. We live in the era of God's mercy, which means nobody dies today for complaining. However, it may keep you out of your promised land – which probably isn't a nation, but may be the dreams of your heart. Psalm 100:4 says, "Enter into His gates with thanksgiving…" The gates leading to a building are usually situated on the boundary of its land. They represent the first threshold that you must cross in order to make your way inside. If you cannot get through the gates, you will not be able to enter the building. Gratitude is essential to entering into God's promises.

Stagnation & Sickness

God gave us the ability to desire as a means of growing hope in our hearts. Hebrews 11:1 says, "Now faith is the substance of things hoped for…" This verse explains that hope becomes faith in the right environment, just as water stored in a freezer becomes ice. Not only that, when we desire God's promises, it propels us to persevere until fulfillment. If we desire what belongs to someone else, it fixes our focus on something that we cannot have. The force that should be pushing us towards our purpose ends up creating a bondage to what we cannot have. It takes our eyes off our promises and onto other people. As a result, longing for something belonging to someone else causes you to get stuck. When you are stuck, you start to stagnate and lose the vitality of life. It is a demonic plot to keep you out of God's best. The Lord wants to set you free so that you can pursue your purpose with joy.

Discontentment saps your energy. Words either bring death or breathe life (Proverbs 18:21). As we already saw, negativity causes discouragement. It not only brings us down, but it affects the people around us too. A few years ago, I brought one of my leaders on a ministry trip. We stayed in various places, as I was ministering in different locations. Unfortunately, nothing seemed to be quite right for my travel companion. The first day, the breakfast was not up to scratch. That night, the air conditioning was not strong enough. When we went to the next venue, it was too cold. Her discontent made her a wearisome companion. Thank God, I was able to address the issue and she was gloriously transformed.

Proverbs 14:30 says, "A sound heart is life to the body, but envy is rottenness to the bones." According to Scripture, envy leads to bone decay. That sounds to me a lot like arthritis or osteoporosis. I'm sure you want to protect your health. If we don't deal with negative emotions like envy, we can open the door to disease. Of course, bone problems aren't always caused by heart issues, but let's make sure we don't give the devil a foothold. The first half of Proverbs 14:30 is full of promise: "A sound heart is life to the body..." As you deal with your heart issues, you can experience physical healing! As the bondages that caused sickness are broken, restoration will flow. We will pray into this together.

A Disease That Spreads

Discontent is infectious. Especially if you are influential, your dissatisfaction will affect the attitudes of others. If you remain happy and calm, others will probably follow suit. If you become upset and irritated, people will catch your attitude. Acts 6:1 (NLT) describes how this disease can spread: "But as the believers rapidly multiplied, there were rumblings of discontent. The Greek-speaking believers complained about the Hebrew-speaking believers, saying that their widows were being discriminated against in the daily distribution of food."

Complaints probably began with one or two, but soon, everyone was unhappy with the situation. Discontent can become bitter, and bitterness infects many. Hebrews 12:15 (MSG) says, "Make sure no-one gets left out of God's generosity. Keep a sharp eye out for weeds of bitter discontent. A thistle or two gone to seed can ruin a whole garden in no time." I'm sure you want to be a force for good. It's time to deal with this disease.

The Bible's Antidotes To This Soul Sickness

We are going to look at three heart habits that will set you free from this energy-sapping destiny blocker. As you change your ways, you will be amazed at the joy and strength that becomes your new normal. Not only that, you will be positioning yourself for God's highest purposes.

A few months ago, I was uncharacteristically downhearted, and it lasted for a few days. "What do you think is the issue?" I asked my husband. "You have a gratitude deficit," he answered almost immediately. I could have argued because I worked hard at thankfulness, but I knew better! Instead, I got into God's presence and started to thank Him. Soon I realized that my gratitude had become mechanical. I was *saying* thank you but I wasn't *feeling* grateful.

I decided to keep thanking God until joy bubbled up inside. Then it happened; I thanked God for The Heart Academy which we had launched at the start of that year. The impact in the lives of participants was more than I could have asked or imagined. Each course changed lives. We ministered to precious people in different nations, because it was delivered virtually. Suddenly, I was overjoyed. I couldn't thank the Lord enough for giving me The Heart Academy. I was full to overflowing with gratitude – and the heaviness was long gone.

The Power Of Gratitude

Heartfelt gratitude generates joy. Nehemiah 8:10b says, "...the joy of the Lord is your strength." So, the joy that comes from gratitude in turn releases inner strength, and it drives out dissatisfaction. It is impossible to be full of joy and discontent. Remember, this must come from your heart, otherwise it is just lip service. If you persevere as I did, you will always find something that stirs genuine gratitude. Thankfulness keeps your spirit light even when everything around you is dark. It has nothing to do with circumstances and everything to do with choices. 1 Thessalonians 5:18 (NLT) says, "Be thankful in all circumstances, for this is God's will for you who belong to Christ Jesus." We don't thank Him *for* everything but we must be grateful *in* every season of life. He is good and deserves our heartfelt thanks.

Not only does a grateful heart open destiny doors, multiple studies show that it improves your quality of life. Thankfulness reduces depression; grateful people sleep better; those who are thankful have higher self-esteem; appreciative folk find it easier to build relationships; and gratitude improves physical health. You must remember that for the research to be valid, they had to compare people facing similar circumstances. The differentiator was how thankful the subjects were, despite their surroundings. We can always decide to be grateful.

The medicine for envy goes a step further; it is intercession and celebration. Pray for the Lord to prosper those who you once envied. Ask God to give them the desires of their hearts and to lead them into His highest plans for their lives. Then celebrate their successes! Rejoice in the blessings that once caused you to be envious. Choose to be glad for the promotions that you once resented. When you are ready to celebrate someone else's breakthrough, you are probably ready to enjoy your own. If you will do this, it will be medicine to your heart, and to your body.

Choose To Remember

We all know people who have it all (or nearly) and yet seem dissatisfied. On the other hand, it is humbling to meet those who are overflowing with joy despite life's difficulties. After God delivered the children of Israel from the Egyptians, He instructed them to instigate an annual feast. And what was the purpose of this party? "This annual festival will be a visible sign to you, like a mark branded on your hand or your forehead. Let the festival remind you always to recite... 'With a strong hand, the Lord delivered you from Egypt.'" (Exodus 13:9) God established an annual convention for one reason alone: so that His people would never forget His goodness. It was so important that they remembered their blessings that the Lord created a public holiday.

So how does that apply to you and me? How many times do we pray for something to happen, or not to happen? When God comes through, we may say thank you but soon forget His kindness. When we turn a corner and times are tough again, we quickly complain. The Lord wants us to make every effort to remember His goodness. When you face a trial, think back to your last testimony. When life is tough, remind yourself of God's goodness. Gratitude opens doors and makes life more enjoyable.

What Would It Take For You To Be Content?

One of the most life-changing habits that I ever developed is contentment. My mood used to be ruled by my circumstances. I thought that it was normal to be influenced by your setting, or even your season. I assumed I had no control over my emotions when I was standing in line behind a slow cashier or sitting in terrible traffic. If I had somewhere to be and I was delayed, I would be grumpy. Lengthy flights or difficult journeys warranted my frustration, or so I thought. If an evening out or an exciting trip was cancelled, I believed I was bound to be grumpy. That is, until I discovered the life-altering power of contentment.

Paul the Apostle explained that he had *learned* the secret of being content in every situation: "...I have learned how to be content (satisfied to the point where I am not disturbed or disquieted) in whatever state I am." (Philippians 4:11 AMP) Notice that he said it was a lesson that he had to *learn*. But once he had mastered this life-skill, it protected him from angst and stress, even in desperate circumstances. It did not come automatically or without effort, but he cracked it. Paul suffered terribly. He was beaten and shipwrecked. He knew what it was to be hungry and hated. Yet in all these things, he enjoyed an inner contentment.

Hebrews 13:5 says, "Be content with such things as you have. For He Himself has said, 'I will never leave you nor forsake you.'" This Scripture explains why we should be content. You and I should be satisfied simply because we have Him! You could put that verse differently: "Surely, I am enough for you?" In other words, when we are discontented, in our hearts we are saying: "Lord, You are not sufficient for me to be happy." Contentment is an expression of our gratitude to God for His presence. He is our reward, our joy, our life.

You are probably not contending with the persecutions that faced Apostle Paul. However, like Paul, we can choose to be content in any and every situation. We can simply maintain our peace, no matter what happens, and smile on the inside. It really is as simple as this. Try it, you will be amazed how you can go through terrible trials without losing your joy. You will be able to experience difficulties and maintain a peaceful inner atmosphere.

From Discontent to Destiny

Godliness alone is not enough to open the door to the abundant life Jesus died to provide. 1 Timothy 6:6b (AMP) says, "... godliness accompanied with contentment (that contentment which is a sense of inward sufficiency) is great and abundant gain." You need to be content in order to enjoy an abundant life. The successful Proverbs 31 woman guarded her home and business against discontent. Proverbs 31:27 (AMP) says, "She looks well to how things go in her household, and the bread of idleness (gossip, discontent, and self-pity) she will not eat." As you grow into the call of God on your life, it will become increasingly important to keep this attitude out of your life.

The way you start is not hugely important, nor is the length of your journey, it is how you finish that makes the difference.

When God was raising up David, the Lord sent men to help His chosen leader. But they were a bit of a mess when they arrived on the scene! 1 Samuel 22:2 (NASB) says, "Everyone who was in distress, and everyone who was in debt, and everyone who was discontented gathered to him; and he became captain over them. Now there were about four hundred men with him." Discontent was rampant among this group of disgruntled men, but they did not remain that way. It is impossible to achieve great things without optimism, faith, and resilience. These gentlemen were changed into selfless warriors who brought victories to the children of Israel. At the time of his death, David called these followers mighty men. Let's pray for God to accomplish that same work in our lives.

Heavenly Father,

I am so sorry for being dissatisfied with my life. I apologize for complaining and getting upset when circumstances were challenging. I allowed the storms and difficulties of life to dictate my mood. I realize my error and I repent today. I want to get all negativity and ingratitude out of my life. Cleanse me, I pray. I easily become irritated and frustrated. I allow all sorts of silly things to wind me up and get me down. I am sorry. Forgive me, Lord.

Father, I have envied the blessings that you have released into the lives of others. I have resented their breakthroughs and promotions. They are Your children, and You alone know their hearts. I have found fault and I have criticized people, which has grieved Your heart. I was wrong to harden inside and react with envy. I am so sorry, Lord. I don't want to react this way ever again. I ask You to forgive me and to change me.

I pray for those I once resented. (*Now pray by name for anyone that you know you have envied.*) I ask You to bless them, refresh them, prepare them for Your highest plans. Bless their families, their ministries, and their work. Open new doors for them, I pray. And thank You for every breakthrough and blessing they have enjoyed! I rejoice at their successes, and I give You glory for their lives.

Today I choose to live a life of thankfulness. (*Now spend a few minutes telling the Lord all the things that you are grateful for. Continue until genuine joy bubbles up inside.*) Help me to be grateful, no matter what is going on around me. Lord, You are enough for me. Help me to be content. Help me to choose contentment every day and in every situation. Help me to foster joy in all circumstances.

I ask for Your healing power to flow into my joints, bones, ligaments, and muscles. I drive out any diseases that took hold because of wrong heart attitudes, and I declare that by the stripes that wounded Jesus, I am healed and made whole. Thank you that my healthy heart will release healing to my body.

I love You with all of my heart, and I am grateful for all You have done and continue to do for me.

In Jesus' name, I pray,

Amen.

Chapter Five

I WANT JUSTICE

I am going to tell you about a young man with a great destiny that I will call Andy. His dad, who I will call Dan, was a community leader who was loved and celebrated by people far and wide. But he was a terrible husband and an awful father. Dan had children from different women and never conquered his problem as a womanizer. It seemed like no lady was off limits: single, married, it was all the same to Dan. Home was not a happy place, but there was one person who meant the world to Andy, and that was his sister, whom I will call Tracy. In the absence of a caring father figure, Andy took on the role of protector to his precious little sister.

As they began to grow up, Andy noticed something that sickened him to the stomach. His eldest brother 'Alistair' was paying Tracy the wrong kind of attention. You can imagine his horror when one day, Tracy ran to Andy's place brokenhearted. Alistair had raped Andy's sister. Certain that their father would punish his firstborn, Andy held his peace. But Dan did nothing. He continued to serve the community and help the people with faultless dedication, yet neglected to defend his daughter Tracy.

Infuriated by his father's failure to seek justice for Tracy, Andy became hellbent on taking vengeance. He hatched a plan, and two years after Alistair raped his beloved sister, Andy destroyed the abuser. Aware that his dad may now lash out at him, Andy quickly packed up his things, collected Tracy, and left town. By this time, Andy was married with his own family. As a tribute to his love for his sister, Andy even named his eldest daughter Tracy.

Three Long Years

It was three years before Dan reached out to Andy, and even then, he didn't come himself. He sent one of his assistants. Although Andy was furious with his dad, like any son, he craved his father's affections. However, instead of love, Andy only received what felt like a cold shoulder. His dad, the 'big leader', sent his team to move Andy and his family back to their hometown. As Andy moved home, he hoped that his father would apologize for his mistakes and that their relationship could be restored. But things only got worse. Dan refused to see his son for two years. The rejection was almost unbearable. By the time Dan agreed to a meeting, it was too late. Andy's heart was hard as stone. He despised his father.

A Man With Many Emotions

If you've heard of Absalom in the Bible, you probably have a dim view of him. But he was a young man who had a difficult upbringing. 'Andy' is Absalom. I told his story to help you see Absalom's humanity. Scripture tells his story so that you and I can tell a different story. Let's look at his life and discover how his response to pain and injustice led to his downfall. The enemy has no new tricks. He just uses old, recyclable tactics to trap you and me.

The devil's most trusted weapon could well be buried pain. You see, hidden hurts lead to countless other problems as varied as pride, low self-worth, discouragement, sickness, and sorrow. One of the chief reasons why the healing of your heart is essential is that the enemy tries to use buried pain to bury you. If you have been mistreated by people who should have known better, ask the Holy Spirit to show you any hurt or anger hiding in your heart. We need to close the door to the devil.

A gifted guy with a great destiny, Absalom was King David's third son, and his mother was the king's third wife. Let's stop there for a moment. 2 Samuel 3:2-3 says, "Sons were born to David in Hebron:

His firstborn was Amnon by Ahinoam the Jezreelitess; his second, Chileab, by Abigail the widow of Nabal the Carmelite; the third, Absalom the son of Maacah, the daughter of Talmai, king of Geshur."

The king's flaws as a husband and father meant that his family saw a very different side to David than what the people saw. Can you imagine what it must have been like knowing that your dad picked up a wife in almost every city? Seeing this same man being celebrated may have stirred anger in Absalom's heart: "You don't see who he really is!" He could have believed that his father was a hypocrite and a fraud.

If you were mistreated by someone who has been publicly appreciated, the sense of injustice may be overwhelming. Perhaps you were wounded by a well-loved leader, maybe you were hurt by a popular family member, you could have been the victim of secret domestic violence. Your story may be different, but the pain of injustice could be all too familiar. Proverbs 20:27 says, "The spirit of a man is the lamp of the Lord, searching all the inner depths of his heart." Please allow the Lord to shine His light into the depths of your heart and heal the hurts buried inside. He is able to restore your soul.

When Tamar was raped by her eldest brother Amnon, Absalom must have been deeply grieved. The fact that he was the person that she turned to illustrates their closeness: "Then Tamar put ashes on her head, and tore her robe of many colors that was on her, and laid her hand on her head and went away crying bitterly. And Absalom her brother said to her, 'Has Amnon your brother been with you? But now hold your peace, my sister. He is your brother; do not take this thing to heart.' So Tamar remained desolate in her brother Absalom's house." (2 Samuel 13:19-20)

Sometimes seeing someone you love suffer can be even more painful than enduring the hardship yourself. The sense of helplessness can be horrific and the grief deep. All too often, the devil suggests that you are responsible, adding guilt to your distress.

Just Do Something!

Absalom must have believed that his dad would hold his firstborn to account and defend his daughter. So, when the king did nothing, the sense of injustice must have burned in his heart. Absalom took matters into his own hands and killed his brother. Afterwards, he left Jerusalem in case his dad came after him. Absalom was gone three years before David sent a servant to bring his son back to Jerusalem. I'm sure the young man hoped for some kind of restoration, but instead he received more rejection.

2 Samuel 14:24 explains, "And the king said, 'Let him return to his own house, but do not let him see my face.' So Absalom returned to his own house, but did not see the king's face." David brought him home but refused to see his son for two long years. When the king eventually felt ready to forgive him, it was too late. Absalom's heart had grown hard. This young man with a promising future judged his dad and decided that he was stained by his mistakes. He came to the conclusion that King David was no longer fit to serve. But only God knows the hearts of His people, only the Lord is able to make that call.

Full of anger, Absalom wanted his father to pay. No doubt, he felt justified in his course of action. Absalom saw himself and his sister as victims of injustice, and he believed his dad was a perpetrator. Absalom wanted his father to suffer, and he believed that he was in the right. So, he hatched a plan. First, he worked to win the affections of the people: "...Absalom stole the hearts of the men of Israel..." (2 Samuel 15:6b) After turning their hearts away from his father, he tried to overthrow the king, his dad. 2 Samuel 15:10 tells the story: "Then Absalom sent spies throughout all the tribes of Israel, saying, 'As soon as you hear the sound of the trumpet, then you shall say, "Absalom reigns in Hebron!"'."

He tried to take the kingdom from David and assert himself as ruler of the people. Absalom attempted to destroy his dad and ended up destroying himself. To me the saddest verse about this young man describes the way that he died: "Absalom rode on a mule. The mule went under the thick boughs of a great terebinth tree and his head caught in the terebinth; so he was left hanging between heaven and earth." (2 Samuel 18:9)

The Destiny Killer

What went on in Absalom's heart that led to such a devastating end? He judged his dad over and over again. Injustice turned this young man with a bright future into a judge. Judgement is when we come to the conclusion, not just that what someone has done is wrong, but that *they* are wrong. This kind of judgement leads to condemnation. Because they are wrong, we decide that they are stained by their transgressions and therefore not fit to serve.

Romans 8:1 says, "There is therefore now no condemnation to those who are in Christ Jesus, who do not walk according to the flesh, but according to the Spirit." The Lord of All chooses to withhold condemnation. But so often, we write people off because of their mistakes. When we judge and condemn, our consciences become seared, and we feel justified. Romans 14:4 warns us that it is never our place to stand as judge: "Who are you to judge another's servant? To his own master he stands or falls. Indeed, he will be made to stand, for God is able to make him stand." The Lord's desire is always to restore you and me after we mess up. And this is also His heart for those who have caused us harm. When we judge, we step into the office reserved for God alone. Only He knows hearts and motives. He sees a much bigger picture than we do. "Oh, the depth of the riches both of the wisdom and knowledge of God! How unsearchable are His judgments and unfathomable His ways!" (Romans 11:33 NASB)

How often do you have thoughts similar to those below? These might not be your exact sentiments, but how likely are you to react in these sorts of ways to what you see or hear?

Score yourself against each sentiment on a scale of 1 (never) to 10 (all the time):

1. Her behavior was appalling. _____

2. He doesn't deserve to be standing on that platform. _____

3. What on earth is that woman wearing? _____

4. I can't believe he would say that. _____

5. What is wrong with her driving? _____

6. That stupid idiot. _____

7. They are only in it for the money. _____

8. She is too slow, it's excruciating. _____

9. He is mean and judgmental _____

10. She deserves everything that's happened _____

Irrespective of whether this is a big issue for you or an occasional habit, the Lord wants to tackle judgement for sake of your destiny.

The Three Responses To Pain

If you have been mistreated, please know that the enemy wants you to judge the one who caused you pain. Once judgement has entered your heart, you may find yourself wishing the worst or secretly celebrating their downfalls. That's because judgement leads us to condemnation. It makes us believe that we are right, and that they are wrong. In truth, when you get hurt, you have three choices. You can either hide from the pain, you can harden towards those who have caused you grief, or you can heal.

Hiding from your pain may sound like a harmless option. Perhaps you have been cut off by people you love. Maybe you endured a life-shattering loss, or you could have been badly treated. Facing pain is distressing, so avoiding it is understandable. However, burying or denying that you've been wounded does not make the pain go away. It gets buried in the recesses of your soul and weighs you down. It chokes the life out of you and dampens your joy. It hampers your relationships and puts a strain on your ability to trust. When you hide from your pain, it hides in your heart and holds you back. It can even shorten your days.

A Hard Heart

The second response to injustice is to harden. If you have suffered, the devil will tempt you to judge those who have hurt you, and when you judge, you harden. He wants you to toughen towards them. A hard heart is a cold, closed heart. It is unfeeling, jaded, and somewhat callous. When you have been wounded, it is all too easy to become hard, but this is dangerous.

Psalm 95:7b-11 reads: "Today, if you will hear His voice: 'Do not harden your hearts, as in the rebellion, as in the day of trial in the wilderness, when your fathers tested Me; they tried Me, though they saw My work. For forty years I was grieved with that generation, and said, "It is a people who go astray in their hearts, and they do not know My ways." So I swore in My wrath, "They shall not enter My rest".'"

This is one of Scripture's saddest passages. The children of Israel hardened their hearts. It grieved God to such an extent that He made an irrevocable decision to keep them from their promised land. We can make mistakes that have consequences. This was different. This heart attitude hurt our Heavenly Father so much that He barred His beloved children from their original inheritance. It is never worth holding judgement. Leave that to our righteous God and instead ask the Lord to heal your precious heart.

You don't have to hide from your pain, and you don't need to be weighed down by a hard heart. There is a third response: you can seek healing. Psalms 147:3 (AMP) says, "He heals the brokenhearted and binds up their wounds [curing their pains and their sorrows]." There is no pain that the Lord can't take away. There is no wound that the Lord can't heal. Tell your Heavenly Father how you have suffered, share what you went through in prayer. Pour out your pain in His presence and ask Him to restore your soul. If you will allow the Lord to heal you every time you are hurt, you will be able to maintain a tender heart.

When The Tables Turn

When God turns your situation around, you may find yourself in a position where you can get your own back for the pain you endured at the hands of others. Have you ever pictured yourself in a place of power over someone who hurt you? Have you craved an opportunity to prove yourself in front of those who criticized your actions or doubted your value? Have you imagined yourself showing them how wrong they were? It feels good to the flesh to fantasize about taking some sort of revenge, even if payback is subtle.

I never cease to be amazed at the example of Joseph. He and his brothers were raised in a God-fearing home by parents who loved the Lord. I'm sure they were told stories about their great-grandfather Abraham's faith in God. They must have known that the birth of their grandad, Isaac, was a miracle and that the God of heaven and earth had a great plan for each of their lives. Joseph's brothers should have known how to behave. Despite a God-fearing upbringing, these men violently turned on their young brother. They attacked Joseph, they stripped him and kicked him into a pit. It didn't stop there. They sold Joseph as though he were an animal (today, we call that human trafficking), which led to thirteen years of slavery and imprisonment.

Such betrayal and brutality gave Joseph every right to seek retribution. It would have been completely justifiable for him to make his brothers pay for their cruelty. Furthermore, the perfect opportunity presented itself. Joseph had it all – position, power, prosperity – and his brothers had nothing. He could have lorded it over them. Yet, right from the start of their reunion, Joseph was gracious.

Joseph's first open exchange with his brothers after they were reunited is recorded in Genesis 45:4-5 (NLT): "'Please, come closer,' he said to them. So they came closer. And he said again, 'I am Joseph, your brother, whom you sold into slavery in Egypt. But don't be upset, and don't be angry with yourselves for selling me to this place. It was God who sent me here ahead of you to preserve your lives.'"

Joseph's first words after the brothers were reunited were designed to reassure. He didn't let them sweat, not even for a moment. But he went even further than that. He informed the men that tried to destroy his life that it was God's doing. He told his brothers that they were not to blame for his terrible suffering. He let them off the hook.

Joseph's Perspective

Even after enjoying many years of peace and prosperity in Egypt, the sons of Jacob worried that Joseph had only been good to them for the sake of their father. When Jacob died, the brothers were terrified that Joseph would take his chance to exact revenge. In fear for their lives and their families, they hatched a plan. The men told Joseph that their dad had instructed them to come after his death to see their brother to ask for forgiveness.

We will pick up the story in Genesis 50:17: "…'Thus you shall say to Joseph: "I beg you, please forgive the trespass of your brothers and their sin; for they did evil to you." Now, please, forgive the trespass of the servants of the God of your father.' And Joseph wept when they spoke to him."

Joseph's response showed the depth of his tenderness towards his betrayers. He broke down and wept. However, what he said in response reveals something that may be even more important. His answer gives us a window into Joseph's perspective. I believe it is this that helped him keep a soft heart towards the men who tried to destroy his destiny. "Joseph said, 'Do not be afraid, for am I in the place of God?'" (Genesis 50:19)

Joseph refused to judge because he believed judgment was God's job. He saw himself as a fellow servant even though he was a lord in the land. He was saying to his siblings, "I don't have the right to judge you." Without even realizing it, he was protecting the purity of his heart. Thousands of years later, Paul the Apostle put it like this: "Who are you to condemn someone else's servants? Their own master will judge whether they stand or fall. And with the Lord's help, they will stand and receive his approval." Romans 14:4 (NLT)

Your Responsibility

Each of us will give an account to God of our words and our works (see Romans 14:12). You and I are not responsible for anyone else's actions. We are accountable for our *own* behavior. We will never have to report to God on how others fared through their ups and downs. If we focus on the failings of others, we are missing the point of much of Scripture. God's heart is always for my restoration when I mess up. He has the same longing for those who have hurt you and me. God never enjoys judgement. He loves releasing His mercy. James 4:12 sums it up: "...Who are you to judge another?"

In truth, we don't know what goes on in the lives of other people. It does not matter how well we are acquainted with someone. Only God knows their hearts. As a result, we are not equipped to assess their attitudes or actions. That's God's job. When someone has hurt me or let me down, my carnal instinct is to judge. This is the thought which has often helped me to climb down from that place: "Until I have lived your life and walked in your shoes, I 'know that I would have behaved any differently."

Let me share again something that happened on the day that our daughter died. My husband and I drove home from the hospital in a daze. We were traveling slowly in the fast lane of the highway. A car drew up behind us and the driver became very impatient. He tooted his horn and shook his fist. Alarmed, we quickly pulled over into the slow lane. I learned an important lesson that day. You never know what is going on in someone else's life. You never know what is causing their behavior.

The Problem With Judgement

The Bible says that when we judge others, we open the door to being judged ourselves: "Do not judge or you too will be judged. For in the same way you judge others, you will be judged and with the measure you use, it will be measured to you." (Matthew 7:1-2) There are not many occasions in Scripture when God says that if we withhold something, He will too. For example, the Bible says that when we are faithless, He remains faithful. However, there is something about setting ourselves up as a critic of a fellow human being that repels the Lord's blessing. If we judge, we will be judged in return.

This is a destiny maker or breaker. As long as we are imperfect, we depend on the mercy of God. I need His mercy to cover my many mistakes and His favor to shine on me despite my shortcomings. I covet the generosity of heart and goodwill of my family and friends. When I fail or slip up (as I often do), I seek their understanding and forgiveness. I need my husband to let me off the hook when I let him down. I want my children to show mercy when I'm short-tempered. I look to my team to be gracious when I get things wrong. To receive mercy from God and people, I need to show mercy to others.

Mercy is being kind to those who don't deserve it. It is showing love when I want to hate. Romans 14:13 (NLT) says, "Let's stop condemning each other..." It must be heartbreaking for our Heavenly Father. He who is rich in mercy towards *all* His children has to witness one of His children criticizing and condemning another. All too often we even turn our judgements into prayers and ask the Lord to punish those who have hurt us. I will never forget a day when I was whining to the Lord about the behavior of a sister. I heard the response of God so clearly: "Oh, be quiet, she has been complaining to me about you as well!" That's the behavior of toddlers, not grown-up believers.

The devil wants you to gloat when those that have hurt you face difficulty or hardship. Proverbs 24:17-18 (AMP) says, "Rejoice not when your enemy falls, and let not your heart be glad when he stumbles or is overthrown, lest the Lord see it and it be evil in His eyes and displease Him, and He turn away His wrath from him [to expend it upon you, the worst offender]."

You might not have enemies as such, but replace the word *enemy* in this verse with the name of someone who has caused you pain. It grieves the Lord when we wish the worst for anyone. God says that gloating over misfortune displeases Him; He calls that attitude evil. In fact, this verse suggests that judgement is a greater offense than the wrong they did. Why? Probably because judgement is God's responsibility; after all, He is the only One who knows the intent of people's hearts.

Matthew 7:1-2 (AMP) is clear: "Do not judge and criticize and condemn others, so that you may not be judged and criticized and condemned yourselves. For just as you judge and criticize and condemn others, you will be judged and criticized and condemned, and in accordance with the measure you [use to] deal out to others, it will be dealt out again to you." If I criticize or condemn someone who has hurt me, I will attract judgement when I miss the mark. The wonderful thing is that breaking the habit of passing judgement is liberating. Criticism stirs anger and unrest.

When you climb down, you protect your peace. When you rein in your reactions, you maintain your joy.

The Judgement Trap

Sophia's father was violent, while her mother was controlling and critical. Sophia was frequently torn apart by her mom's cruelty as she used her words like weapons. Gloriously saved in her late teens, Sophia joined a local church where she wholeheartedly served the Lord. However, she struggled to get past her childhood. Living nearby, Sophia often saw her parents, but her visits always ended up with arguments. Sophia couldn't stand the way her mother tiptoed around her father's outbursts, despising what Sophia saw as weakness. Despite godly counsel, Sophia never learned to honor her mother.

Fast forward 15 years, Sophia married and became a mother to two beautiful girls: Maria and Isabella. But from early on in Maria's life, Sophia struggled to connect with her eldest daughter. Animosity between the two grew as Maria got older. Even though Sophia wanted to be a loving mother, she found herself cutting her daughter to size on a daily basis. Although she treasured Isabella, she was almost always upset with Maria. The home was filled with strife as Sophia treated her daughter the very same way she was once treated.

Have you ever wondered why so many end up becoming just like a parent they detested? One of the reasons is rooted in the power of judgement. Romans 2:1 (AMP) explains: "...in posing as judge and passing sentence on another, you condemn yourself, because you who judge are habitually practicing the very same things [that you censure and denounce]." If you hold a parent (or indeed anyone) in judgement, you unwittingly set yourself a trap that binds you into the very behavior you despise. You become what you judge.

The Problem With Parents

I am yet to meet a perfect parent. Even the most wonderful fathers and mothers make frequent mistakes. Then there are the many wounded moms and dads that struggle to get anything right. Maybe your father was absent, and you grew up without his love or affirmation. Perhaps your dad was harsh or distant. It could be your mother that hurt you the most. Cruel comments, constant comparison, or coldness. I believe that everyone has been damaged in some way by their parents. After all, it's a huge job, carried out by imperfect people.

Any time you are hurt, there will be a temptation to judge. Although all people are equal, not all judgement is equal. Let me explain. Ephesians 6:2-3 says, "Honor your father and mother," which is the first commandment with promise: "that it may be well with you and you may live long on the earth." God promises long life and wellbeing to those who honor their parents. Dishonor, in contrast, opens the door to difficulty. God is not interested in lip service; He looks at your heart. Isaiah 29:13b says, "...these people draw near with their mouths and honor Me with their lips, but have removed their hearts far from Me..." It is impossible to judge and honor at the same time. So judging your parents is costly. It attracts the judgement of others and jeopardizes your wellbeing. Being healed of every hurt makes graciousness so much easier.

The Mirror Of God

Standing on the front row at a packed conference, I was overwhelmed by the closeness of God. It was in that precious atmosphere that the Holy Spirit held up a mirror to my heart: "Stop judging My servants." Suddenly aware of an appalling, yet unconscious habit, I apologized to the Lord. I don't know how I slipped into such unpleasant thought patterns, but I would often size up ministers as I decided if I wanted to listen to their message.

I immediately understood how much my haughty opinions had grieved the Lord. Who was I to evaluate the worth of a minister of God?

1 Corinthians 14:29 (AMP) instructs us to assess what we are hearing: "So let two or three prophets speak [those inspired to preach or teach], while the rest pay attention and weigh and discern what is said." Weighing what is said is very different to judging a speaker. It is important that you and I consider what we are being taught. Acts 17:11 (NIV) says, "Now the Berean Jews were of more noble character than those in Thessalonica, for they received the message with great eagerness and examined the Scriptures every day to see if what Paul said was true." The Bereans weighed up the words Paul spoke and readily received the truth. They did not judge Paul.

Social media has made it seem acceptable to vocalize opinions about preachers. They are on public display, so it is natural to work out what you think of a teaching. But we need to be careful not to allow our opinions to become public (or private) accusations. God calls Satan the accuser of the brethren (see Revelation 12:10), so that job is already taken. We need to make sure that nothing we say or do could harm a minister. I think it is fair to say that if you or I damage a preacher's reputation, we are harming them.

You don't need to agree with every teacher, and you certainly don't need to celebrate everyone. But 1 Chronicles 16:22 is clear: "Do not touch My anointed ones, and do My prophets no harm." Let's back down from judgement and keep our hearts humble, especially when it comes to ministers. When the Lord calls a man or woman into ministry, He calls them *His* servant. Romans 14:4 says, "Who are you to judge another's servant? To his own master he stands or falls. Indeed, he will be made to stand, for God is able to make him stand." God is able to manage His staff without our help. And His heart is that every one of His servants succeeds.

1 Timothy 2:1-2 says, "I urge, then, first of all, that petitions, prayers, intercession and thanksgiving be made for all people – for kings and all those in authority…" Instead of criticizing, let's pray.

I Want Justice!

Have you ever cried out to God for justice? Have you told friends or family that you're not asking for revenge, but you want justice? I will never forget the day my husband warned me of the dangers of asking God for justice. You see, I can't ask God to give others what they deserve and then plead with Him to overlook my shortcomings. Without his mercy, I would be doomed. Psalms 130:3 (MSG) says, "If you, God, kept records on wrongdoings, who would stand a chance?"

I don't want the Lord to treat me according to my mistakes; I don't want to reap a harvest for my errors. I'm sure you don't want that either. If you want to depend upon the mercy of God every time you mess up, then it's time to lay down any quest for justice. God is rich in mercy; He is also just. Deuteronomy 32:4 describes His nature: "He is the Rock, His work is perfect; for all His ways are justice, a God of truth and without injustice; righteous and upright is He." He knows how to weigh actions and motives. He will always do what is right.

While you are eaten up inside by the sense of being wronged, there will be a well of negativity swilling around in your soul. It will grip your attention and it will drain your joy. Random experiences around you will remind you of what went wrong. One of the reasons that the devil attempts to keep us in judgement is that it can keep us out of God's purposes for our lives.

The Toxic Mix

Just as cakes are made of flour, eggs, butter, and sugar, judgement is made up of a few core ingredients: pride, accusation, and condemnation. When I assess the actions of a fellow human being, I am putting myself in the place of God, but judgement is God's job because He knows the hearts of His people. When I judge, I suggest that I know best. Remember Joseph's words of reassurance to his brothers in Genesis 50:19: "Do not be afraid, for am I in the place of God?" Despite being in a position of power, Joseph understood he had no right to judge the men who tried to destroy him; he understood he was merely human. When we judge, we put ourselves in the place of God. Pride has entered our hearts. God hates pride so much that He will push us away while we are in that state. James 4:6b says, "God resists the proud, but gives grace to the humble."

The Holy Spirit is an Encourager. He uses the Word of God to lift our spirits when times are tough. In contrast, Satan is the accuser of the brethren. Judgement, by definition, has an air of accusation. We look at the shortcomings of a brother or sister and indict them in our hearts. We take up that enemy mandate to lay charges at their feet. This is not the behavior God wants from believers.

Judgement also involves condemnation. When I judge, I call for a culprit to be held to account and to be made to pay for their shortcomings. The Holy Spirit never condemns believers, He convicts them. Condemnation is the enemy's role, so if I write off one of God's children, I am doing the devil's dirty work. In contrast, Romans 8:1 (NLT) says, "So now there is no condemnation for those who belong to Christ Jesus." When I condemn someone, I am coming against part of the plan of salvation. I am operating from a very different spirit to the generosity of the Holy Spirit.

Have You Been Judged?

Have you been hurt by the judgements of others? Perhaps family or friends pointed the finger, blaming you for circumstances beyond your control? Maybe you have been winded by cruel assumptions. Proverbs 12:18 explains, "There is one who speaks like the piercings of a sword..." It is not just physical attacks that can cut. Harsh words can tear you up inside. You could have been judged as a result of old mistakes. Maybe you feel that your errors will follow you wherever you go. God wants to heal the bruising that condemnation can cause. He wants to take your pain away.

Lamentations 2:19b explains what we are supposed to do with our pain: "Pour out your heart like water before the face of the Lord..." When you pour out your heart to a friend, you share your deepest issues. This usually brings a measure of relief. When you share your secret hurts with your Wonderful Counsellor (one of the names given to Jesus in Isaiah 9:6), He listens attentively then reaches into the depths of your heart and heals.

If you feel judged, please don't carry that pain any longer. Set aside some time to talk to the Lord about what you have been through. Share how those experiences made you feel. King David knew how to give the pain of judgement to the Lord. In Psalms 64:3 (NLT), he told God, "They sharpen their tongues like swords and aim their bitter words like arrows." David often wept in God's presence as he shared his heart. In the same way, as you release buried pain before the Lord, He will restore your soul.

The Cruelty Of Criticism

Criticism might be common, but it is not harmless. Proverbs 12:18 (MSG) says, "Rash language cuts and maims..." Harsh comments can make you feel like a failure, they can cause you to doubt yourself. Unkind criticism can open the door to discouragement. The Bible compares verbal attacks with a lethal weapon. Proverbs 12:18 (TPT) says, "Reckless words are like the thrusts of a sword, cutting remarks meant to stab and to hurt..."

Have there been times when you put your whole heart into your efforts, but were made to feel like you failed? Maybe your parents put you down irrespective of how hard you tried. Perhaps your spouse or boss cross-examined your best attempts. If you have been wounded by words, the Lord wants to heal your heart. Ephesians 6:16 calls words 'fiery darts'. If you have been crushed by criticism or cut to the heart by angry words, please bring every hurtful comment to the Lord in prayer.

Criticism enters your heart by words, so it needs to be removed the same way. Tell the Lord what was said and how it made you feel. Picture the Lord pulling those 'darts' out of your heart. Continue sharing your pain in prayer until you feel the words have been dislodged. After you have released hurtful comments, allow the healing balm of God's Word to fill your soul. Search the Bible for a Scripture that reveals God's heart towards you. Meditate on His love and acceptance. Ezekiel 3:10b says, "...Receive into your heart all My words that I speak to you..." Allow the Lord's affirmation to sink deep into your soul.

A good verse to mull over is Deuteronomy 7:6: "For you are a holy people to the Lord your God; the Lord your God has chosen you to be a people for Himself, a special treasure above all the peoples on the face of the earth." The Lord has picked you because He loves you and He calls you His special treasure.

Please Don't Lash Back

There is a temptation when you're under fire to fight back. When people judge, the flesh wants to point the finger at your accuser in retaliation. Remember, while God wants to heal your heart, the devil wants you to harden. Any time someone judges you, please give God your anger and forgive. Don't let the devil drag you into judgement through the back door. Let me repeat what I have already said: when we judge, we act as umpire without knowing the facts. Only God knows hearts. Only God knows what happens behind closed doors. So only God is qualified to judge.

Let's look at Joseph's story again. When his brothers fell on their knees and begged him to forgive them years after they tried to destroy his life, this is how he replied: "Do not be afraid, for am I in the place of God?" (Genesis 50:18) Joseph knew that he was not qualified to judge, but he went a step further. Genesis 50:21 tells us that he ministered tenderly to his brothers: "He comforted them and spoke kindly to them." What an example of humility and love.

History Repeating Itself

When you have been hurt by wounding words, the enemy wants to trap you into speaking harshly over others. If you were raised in an atmosphere of anger and judgement, you may find that you have a propensity to be harsh, even with those that you love. As you allow the Lord to restore you, your reflexes will soften. You will be changed from the inside out. However, it's important that we work on ourselves while we are being transformed by the Lord.

Remember what Matthew 7:1 (AMP) says, "Do not judge and criticize and condemn others, so that you may not be judged and criticized and condemned yourselves." The definition of criticize is to find fault. It is easy to find fault. We all make mistakes, so there are plenty of opportunities for us to criticize one another. Anyone can point out flaws and put people down. But, as we have discussed, criticism can feel like an attack. All too often, we have no idea how we come across to others. I remember seeing a good friend shout at her son. When I asked her about it afterwards, she was sure she had spoken firmly but calmly. She was mistaken.

Ask the Lord to show you if you are prone to finding fault in others. You could vocalize your criticism or even keep it in your heart. You may find fault with slow cashiers in shops; it could be waiting staff, family, or co-workers. Proverbs 11:17 (MSG) says, "When you're kind to others, you help yourself; when you're cruel to others, you hurt yourself." Remember, when we deal out criticism, it will come back. But as this verse says, when we are kind, we benefit. If you realize you often criticize, ask the Lord to show you any patterns. Make a point of showing patience towards those you once found frustrating. You will be amazed at how good you feel when you are kind!

You Don't Need To Prove Yourself

A courtroom judge examines the accused in order to determine their innocence or guilt, while the accused attempts (usually with legal help) to prove their innocence. Any time I demand (either openly or in my heart) that someone prove themselves, I am acting as an umpire. I am setting myself up as their judge. Of course, there may be occasions when you need to ask the Lord if it is appropriate for you to trust someone. If you approach God with a humble heart, He will answer your prayers. However, assessing someone to decide if they are 'guilty as charged' is dangerous. Proverbs 18:17 (TPT): "There are two sides to every story. The first one to speak sounds true until you hear the other side and they set the record straight."

Mark 8:11-12 describes an encounter between Jesus and the Pharisees: "Then the Pharisees came out and began to dispute with Him, seeking from Him a sign from heaven, testing Him. But He sighed deeply in His spirit, and said, 'Why does this generation seek a sign? Assuredly, I say to you, no sign shall be given to this generation.'" The Pharisees were testing Jesus. They were assessing his words and actions to bring a charge against Him. Such a heart attitude caused Jesus to be grieved. It's too easy to find yourself eyeing up an acquaintance, cross-examining their motives in your heart. Without all the facts, and with no idea what is in someone else's heart, we decide their innocence or guilt. Let's be careful to avoid such a heart posture.

Your Influence

Jesus warned His disciples to be watchful: "Then He charged them, saying, 'Take heed, beware of the leaven of the Pharisees and the leaven of Herod.'" (Mark 8:15) One dictionary definition of leaven is 'an element that causes expansion or produces an altering influence'. Leaven is yeast. When added to bread, yeast makes it rise. When added to certain liquids, yeast altars the taste and composition, it turns certain liquids into alcohol. Among other things, leaven is a metaphor for influence.

The Pharisees and Herodians were poisoning the Jews, they were contaminating people's opinions of Jesus. Words are seeds. If someone takes my words to heart, what I have said will affect their beliefs and opinions. When you have been hurt by someone's actions, it can be tempting to use your influence to prejudice the opinions of others towards the perpetrator. Let's be careful to use our influence for good.

When you fall short, I'm sure you want help to find your way back. I'm sure you want people to be kind. Matthew 7:12 explains how you can attract kindness when you need it the most: "Therefore, whatever you want men to do to you, do also to them, for this is the Law and the Prophets." The laws of sowing and reaping affect every area of our lives. Let's use our influence in loving and uplifting ways.

The Ingredients Of Mercy

The opposite of judgement is mercy. The first ingredient of mercy is humility. When you have a humble heart, it is easier to climb down from judgement and show people the same graciousness that you have received from God. Philippians 2:3b-4 (NLT) says, "...Be humble, thinking of others as better than yourselves. Don't look out only for your own interests, but take an interest in others, too." If I really see myself as a servant, I won't think it is my place to judge anyone.

Humility is more attainable when you know your value. Knowing He was a Son, Jesus became a servant (see Philippians 2:5-8). Serving does not make a secure person feel worthless. If you have a low opinion of yourself, the Lord wants you to stay on your healing journey. He wants to reach into the depths of your heart and heal you of every painful experience that made you feel unworthy. My book, *My Whole Heart*, will help you on this journey. Also, check out our Heart Academy courses at JoNaughton.com.

Perhaps you were raised by parents who constantly put you down. "You idiot!" they may have hollered every time you got something wrong. You could have suffered from an affection deficit. God designed your soul for fellowship. He formed your inward being for the giving and receiving of love. As a result, the human heart is intensely absorbent, fashioned to soak up love. If you grew up in a cold atmosphere, where you felt tolerated more than celebrated, you may have developed a deep-seated dislike for yourself.

You are precious because you belong to Jesus. You can be perfectly secure in God. That comes when you are convinced of your worth to your Heavenly Father and when you know how much He values you. Out of the knowledge that you are a joint heir with Jesus, you can humble yourself and serve others.

Everyday Attitudes

How we live our everyday lives is of utmost importance to the Lord. I never really thought that I was judgmental. When it came to the big issues, I could show mercy and compassion. If a friend fell flat on her face, I would want to help her back up again, knowing it could easily have been me. In contrast, if someone made silly mistakes, it would wind me up. In truth, I did not believe that this was a problem. I liked competence and thought that expressing intolerance was part of my personality. Although occasionally being abrupt was undesirable, I thought it was part of life. Then God put a yearning in my heart to be tender. It was easy for me to be tough, but God is also tender. Tenderness is the second ingredient of mercy. Colossians 3:12 says, "Therefore, as the elect of God, holy and beloved, put on tender mercies, kindness, humility, meekness…" Tenderness is something we put on. It is something we do.

Mercy works with tenderness, just as judgement works with harshness. When I am annoyed, I am reacting to a judgement I have made. For example, if someone is late for a meeting and I am annoyed, I am taking on the role of their examiner. I'm questioning their competence or professionalism. My assessment of them makes me think that I have the right to be upset: they are below the standard which is required. In contrast, mercy considers their needs and their feelings first. When I am tender, it is a sign that mercy is flowing. When I am harsh, it suggests judgement is rearing its ugly head.

The Way To Graciousness

Judgement is the way to leave the realm of grace. Mercy is the method of entry. Both are doors. One leads us to favor and mercy. The other leads us to a place where we get what we deserve. When my son was growing up, he would often tell his sister about her flaws. When he did this, I would often ask him, "Are you her mum? If the day comes when you are her boss, then feel free to point out her failings. Until then, please build her up." In the same way, God is the head of His big family, so it is His responsibility, not ours, to deal with faults and failings.

Mercy feels good. Sometimes it's hard to get going, but once you're in the flow, it's liberating. While judgement harbors anger and drains your joy, mercy generates joy and releases life. It helps to remove strife and tension from your heart and makes room for patience and understanding. Also, the more mercy you show, the more you will receive from God *and* people.

Matthew 5:7 says, "Blessed are the merciful for they shall obtain mercy." Blessed means happy, so the happiest people on earth are those who are kind and gracious. As we draw this chapter to a close, I will lead you in two prayers. James 5:16 (AMP) says,

"Confess to one another therefore your faults (your slips, your false steps, your offenses, your sins) and pray [also] for one another, *that you may be healed and restored [to a spiritual tone of mind and heart].*"

First, we will come to God and ask Him to heal the pain of injustice and criticism, then we will ask for His help to get judgement out of our lives.

Heavenly Father,

I have gone through so much. The way I have been treated has been unjust and it has hurt me. People that I loved and trusted have let me down. It's not been fair and it hurt me badly. (*Now tell the Lord exactly what you have gone through and how it has made you feel. Share in as much detail as possible.*) At times, I have felt judged. It has been painful and it has worn me down. People have accused me of wrong motives and they have called out my mistakes. It hurt me, Lord. But I don't want to run away from my pain any longer. I don't want to harden inside, so Lord, I ask You to heal my heart. (*Continue telling the Lord what you have gone through and how it has made you feel. Share in as much detail as possible.*)

Lord, I ask You to reach into the depths of my heart and heal, take my pain away, and fill me with Your wonderful love. Thank You, Lord, that You chose me, You picked me, I am Your special treasure. I receive Your wonderful love into the depths of my heart.

Today, I choose to forgive the people who have wronged me, just as You always forgive me my mistakes. (*Now tell the Lord who you are forgiving, explain what they did to hurt you or someone you love, then tell the Lord that you let it go, tell God you release them. Finally, ask Him to bless them, if they are still alive.*)

I realize that I have judged people around me. I have judged those who let me down and I have judged people I hardly know. I ask for Your forgiveness, Lord. I don't want to find fault and criticize anymore, so I climb down from that high place, I humble myself as a servant. Instead of judging, I choose to clothe myself with mercy. I choose to be gracious. I will be tender towards the people around me. I ask for Your help to rid myself of all judgement. Holy Spirit, I ask You to show me any time my thoughts or actions are harsh or accusatory.

I thank You that You always show me mercy, so I will seek to show others the same kindness that You show me.

In Jesus' name I pray,

Amen.

Chapter Six

FREEDOM FROM FEAR

For years, I was controlled by fear. I worried what people thought of me. At dinner parties, nervous energy would make me even louder than usual. Driving home afterwards, I would churn inside wishing I hadn't said what I had said, concerned about how I had come across. If I upset a leader, I would be anxious until I had sorted things out. If my husband was impatient, I would be scared that he didn't love me anymore. Then there was the fear of horses which gripped me any time I was in the countryside, a dread of driving on the 'right' side of the road in America, and I was a very jumpy passenger. Every time fear took hold, I reacted. It had a fierce grip on my life.

Fear is a bully. It creeps up unseen and grips its victims. You may feel a punch in the guts. Perhaps your heart races, or you jump in fright. Maybe your stomach churns or you get overwhelmed. The aim of fear is control. Fear wants you to follow its instructions. They aren't spoken; they are conveyed through threats heard by your heart. "Everyone will laugh at you." "We are going to smash into that car." "It's going to bite." "It's bad news." or "You will make a complete fool of yourself." Fear infers that disaster is imminent and compels you to react.

Do you gasp, wide-eyed, when the car in front brakes? Does your heart race when you see a call from that number? Do you shriek at the sight of rats, snakes, or spiders? Do you clench the steering wheel when you're driving on the highway? Do you avoid public speaking even though you have something to say? Is there one person who you can't bear upsetting? Do you worry what people think of you?

Does the blood drain from your face as you read the bad news? Do you turn crimson when you find yourself in the spotlight?

Who Is In Control?

Fear pushes for a reaction. It wants to bombard your emotions and influence your decisions. Let me repeat myself: fear wants to control you. Romans 8:14 (TPT) says, "The mature children of God are those who are moved by the impulses of the Holy Spirit." More often than not, the Holy Spirit leads with a "still small voice" (see 1 Kings 19:12). He impresses His will upon your heart and then confirms it with an inner calm.

Colossians 3:15 (AMP) says, "And let the peace (soul harmony which comes) from Christ rule (act as umpire continually) in your hearts [deciding and settling with finality all questions that arise in your minds, in that peaceful state] to which as [members of Christ's] one body you were also called [to live] ..." God wants to lead you by His Spirit and confirm His will with an inner peace. Enjoying daily calm is wonderful and it makes it easy to discern God's will. When peace reigns, you know you are on the right path; when discomfort arises, you know to check with God what's wrong. This kind of life is available to every one of us.

Fear wants to take charge instead. It is an enemy of the Holy Spirit, and it fights your destiny. The fact that fear is common can lead us into complacency. Perhaps you have struggled with anxiety for as long as you can remember. Maybe you've always worried what people think. You could have been a jumpy passenger for much of your life. You may have been terrified of dogs since the day you were bitten. Or you could see fear all around: at work, at home, even at church. "Give me a break, everyone is scared of something!" you might say.

It is true that fear is all around. However, it does not change the fact that fear is an enemy of your destiny. If you want to fulfill the call of God on your life, you must conquer *all* your fears. If you give the devil an inch, he will take a mile. If you give him a foothold, he will build a stronghold. To defeat this enemy, you need to develop a zero-tolerance policy. Stop for a moment before you read any further. Ask the Holy Spirit to highlight any fears that are hindering your life. I'm sure you are conscious of some fears, but others may be operating beneath the radar. Ask yourself the questions below to uncover hidden issues.

☐ Do you worry what people think of you?

☐ Do you crave the approval of key people?

☐ Is there someone you can't bear upsetting?

☐ Do you avoid speaking even when you have something to say?

☐ Do you dislike being misunderstood or mocked?

☐ Do you feel anxious in social settings?

☐ Do you get panic attacks?

☐ Are you afraid of failing or being rejected?

☐ Does your heart race when you see a call from certain numbers?

☐ Do you get intimidated by strong people?

☐ Do you turn crimson when you're in the spotlight?

☐ Are you a nervous passenger?

☐ Do you get anxious driving at night, passing trucks or on highways?

☐ Do you grab the steering wheel when the car in front brakes?

☐ Are you afraid of spiders, dogs, snakes, rats, or other creatures?

☐ Are you wary on planes, trains, buses, or bikes?

☐ Do you dislike sudden, loud noises?

☐ Do you feel nervous in unknown settings?

☐ Do certain towns, places, or names cause concern?

☐ Are you afraid of public speaking?

☐ Do you battle with any other fear?

If you answer yes to any of these questions, the Lord wants to set you free from this destiny blocking enemy. He does not want you to be afraid of anything. Open your heart as you read and allow the Lord to transform you from the inside out.

Fear wears many disguises. Do you feel agitated before important events? Are you apprehensive about the future? Do you get anxious in certain settings? Do you feel concerned when things don't go to plan? Do you lie awake worrying? Do you dread injections, sitting exams, or visiting the dentist? Does the prospect of public speaking give you the jitters? Are you timid? Do you panic at bad news? We can use a variety of vocabulary, but all these are forms of fear. And they are all distressing. 1 John 4:18 explains that: "...fear involves torment..." Torment is so disturbing that it makes you react. Depending on what caused the anguish, you will usually either fret, freeze, or flee.

The Problem With Fretting

Fretting is exhausting. Maybe you agonize over what you said or wish you could undo what has been done. Perhaps you're afraid that you offended that all-important person. You could dread an interview, examination, or a crucial meeting. Nagging thoughts steal your peace and drain your energy. The challenge that needs your faith becomes an object of dread.

Proverbs 12:25 (AMP) says, "Anxiety in a man's heart weighs it down..." Worry can be subtle, and at times it can be confused with caring. But worry is rooted in fear. Unfortunately, there is much to worry about: bills, marriage, children, job, exams, health, family.

The list could go on. Perhaps there is always something bothering you, something churning around on the inside. Maybe you are fairly calm until pressure builds, then you become apprehensive. Your sleep is disrupted and your mind whirrs until circumstances change. Once life is back to normal, you are OK. Or you may continue fairly normally through life's many ups and downs, but with nagging thoughts at the back of your mind wearing you out.

The question we need to ask ourselves is whether fretting ever helps. Matthew 6:27 says, "Which of you by worrying can add one cubit to his stature?" It is amazing the things that will bother us if we let them. You can spend a night rehearsing every possible outcome, but your problems will still be there in the morning. In fact, they will probably seem bigger because you are exhausted. Fretting is not just unhelpful. It is harmful.

Luke 8:14 (AMP) says, "And as for what fell among the thorns, these are [the people] who hear, but as they go on their way they are choked and suffocated with the anxieties and cares and riches and pleasures of life, and their fruit does not ripen (come to maturity and perfection)." Worry suffocates faith. Your mind spins and your stomach turns itself into knots. Perhaps you picture the worst. Maybe you become irritable. You do not pray to God – you panic to Him.

Nagging Thoughts

Alternatively, it might just be a nagging thought. But the concern builds and dominates your thoughts or conversation. Irrespective of how it may affect you or me, it always attempts to choke the Word of God out of us. When we are worrying, we are not believing God. The problem has usually become bigger in our minds than the Problem-Solver. That is never the answer.

Philippians 4:6 (AMP) says, "Do not fret or have any anxiety about anything..." There is nothing you face that warrants your worry. 1 Peter 5:7 (AMP) shows you what to do with every concern: "Casting the whole of your care [all your anxieties, all your worries, all your concerns, once and for all] on Him, for He cares for you affectionately and cares about you watchfully."

God not only cares about every issue that you face. He has the power to make a difference. When I was learning to live without constant concern, I developed a daily 'care-casting' habit. I would quieten myself in God's presence. Then I would name every single issue that was worrying me. One by one, I would tell God why I was bothered and then cast each care onto the Lord. I would see myself throwing each problem into God's hands. The load would lighten. Then as I prayed, it would lift entirely. By the end of my session, I would be relieved and refreshed.

Frozen By Fear

I will never forget the night of April 3rd, 2000. My two-year-old daughter had been fighting a cold at the weekend but woke up that Monday morning feeling much better. Naomi enjoyed a lovely day out with her dad but quickly went downhill in the evening. I thought that it might be a long night, so I suggested that my husband slept on the couch. My little girl lay in the bed beside me growing gradually worse. She seemed feverish but had no temperature. Clearly feeling distressed, Naomi kept crawling onto my tummy, wanting to be as close to me as possible.

I could tell that something was very wrong. As the hours passed and Naomi got worse, I began to think that my little girl needed to go to the hospital. But I lay in bed frozen by fear. I was afraid of causing a commotion in the middle of the night. Even though I became convinced that Naomi needed medical help, I did nothing. Fear paralyzed me. I wish there was a happy ending to this story but there isn't. By the time our little girl reached the hospital, she was already very sick and passed away less than 24 hours later.

Perhaps fear has caused you to keep quiet when you knew you had something to say. Maybe fear of failure kept you from applying for a promotion. You could have delayed seeking help because you were concerned about sharing your problem. Perhaps you have received words of encouragement for fellow believers but have been afraid to share. Fear aims to keep you bound. It wants to prevent you from stepping into God's purposes.

Fear Of Human Opinion

Proverbs 29:25 (MSG) says, "The fear of human opinion disables…" When you're afraid of what others think or concerned about someone's reactions, dread makes you hold back when you should step out. For two-thirds of my life, I was preoccupied with the opinions of people. I would worry about what I had said. I would be anxious if I thought I had said too much or too little. If I thought I had upset someone or given the wrong impression, I would lie awake at night, turning it over in my mind.

Proverbs 29:26 says, "Many seek the ruler's favor, but justice for man comes from the Lord." Many means large numbers of the population. It is a word that is used to refer to multitudes. It means most people. The implication is that the majority of us struggle with people-pleasing. I suggest you hold up your hands and ask the Lord to set you free. Seeking the ruler's favor means trying to win the approval of those people who are important to you.

That might be a boss, your spouse, a friend, your father, or even a leader. It is that person whose opinion means everything. When they are happy, all is well. However, when they disapprove of what you are doing or saying, you are distressed. You will do whatever it takes to regain their favor, even if that means changing your plans or opinions. The word favor literally means face. You look to see their reactions and hope for an encouraging smile or an approving nod. When you secure their support, all is well. This is known as people-pleasing, and it is a trap.

Proverbs 29:25 (NLT) says, "Fearing people is a dangerous trap…" A trap binds you. It keeps you from moving forward.

Maybe a stern glance across the room or a challenging question can make you cave in. The thought that you might have offended someone important could fill you with dread. You may end up doing whatever is necessary to try to win back their approval. Fear saps your strength and makes you easy for the enemy to control. You should not be scared of upsetting anyone, if it is for the right reasons. Honoring others is important, but you should never allow fears about their possible reaction to determine your decisions.

Swallowed Up By Fear

Martina became increasingly self-conscious as a teenager. She would shrivel up inside if teachers put her down. As the years went by, she grew afraid of all authority figures. By the time Martina reached adult life, she had become a very timid lady. She ran from any prospect of recognition or responsibility and tried to hide in the shadows. She didn't like meeting new people, especially if they were important. That was just the way she was, or so she thought.

When Martina attended our conference, Healed for Life, she felt as though a mirror was being held in front of her face. She had always thought of herself as a reserved person, never realizing that she had been crippled by fear. Harsh discipline by her father had made her terrified of making mistakes. Public humiliation at junior school had crushed her confidence. God healed the hurts hidden in Martina's heart.

With new courage, Martina realized that if she was going to fulfill God's plans for her life, she would have to deal with this giant. She joined others at our conference and declared: "From this day, I will obey God, not fear. I will seek His approval, not man's!" She continued fighting fear until it lost its power over her. Today, Martina is a phenomenal worship leader at a major city church.

Fleeing Because Of Fear

Fear makes people fret, it causes us to freeze, and it often makes folk flee. The threat of pain makes you run from danger or reach out for relief. That might mean grabbing the car seat, sprinting away from a dog, backing off from that challenge, or shutting your mouth. You could hide from the spotlight, cross the road to avoid certain people, or refuse to travel by plane. I hope that you are beginning to see the cruel way that fear directs people's lives.

Do you remember the story of the Philistine giant Goliath? Every day, this giant strutted in front of the army of Israel, flouting his might and stature. He spouted words of intimidation intended to make the soldiers tremble. Goliath is much like the objects of dread that you and I face. They look larger than life and whisper threats. Overcome by fear, the Israeli soldiers ran from the battle. God had called them to victory but fear caused them to flee. 1 Samuel 17:24 says, "And all the men of Israel, when they saw the man, fled from him and were dreadfully afraid."

The soldiers displayed the greatest source of fear: they were afraid of dying. If you trace back many of your anxieties, they will trace back to the fear of death. Hebrews 2:14b-15 explains what Jesus accomplished when He conquered Satan: "...that through death He might destroy him who had the power of death, that is, the devil, and release those who through fear of death were all their lifetime subject to bondage." We need to conquer the fear of our own death, and we need to break the fear of loved ones dying.

We are going to look at several vital steps to destroying fear's power in our lives. Firstly, we will deal with the doors fear uses to enter our lives. We will then learn how to dismantle fear's power. We will break intimidation; we will discover the right way to respond to triggers. We will find out how much God has already given us, and finally, we will take authority over the spirit of fear.

Different fears may need different solutions, so listen to the Holy Spirit as you read the next few pages. A comprehensive understanding of how to conquer fear will arm you with the weapons you need to win every battle.

1. Who Or What Opened The Door?

Any time the brake lights unexpectedly flashed on the car in front, I would call with a fright, "Paolo!" (that's what I call my husband) while grabbing my car seat with both hands. If a big truck passed close by our car, my heart would pound. For as long as I could remember, I was a nervous passenger, but in truth, I hadn't really realized it. Two issues blinded me to this fear. Firstly, I blamed my anxiety on the drivers who were giving me a ride! Because my husband does much of the driving in my family, I subconsciously attributed my nervousness to my husband's driving!

Until you and I own our fears, we cannot conquer them. While we blame our anxiety on someone else, we give up our power to win the victory. If you realize that you have blamed your nerves on someone else, make a note about that now. It is vital that we accept full responsibility for the condition of our own hearts. Proverbs 4:23 (AMP) says, "Keep and guard your heart with all vigilance and above all that you guard, for out of it flow the springs of life." It is clear from this verse that your heart is your responsibility.

There is a second reason I was unaware that I was a nervous passenger. It was my normal. I had been anxious for as long as I could remember, so I was accustomed to my fears. I was comfortable being afraid. Maybe you have grown so used to worrying that you don't realize it is a problem. The good news is this: you will experience an extraordinary sense of relief, even when invisible burdens are lifted.

After years of accommodating fear, I suddenly noticed that my daughter, Abby, was overly anxious on the roads. The truth slapped me in the face: Abby had 'caught' my nervousness in the car. Like several other heart issues, fear is contagious. A father who is terrified of dogs can pass that on to their child. A teenager can share their fear of exams with their friends. I had given Abby a fear of crashing. I apologized to the Lord for passing on anxiety.

Dealing With The Root

We enter a house through the door. In the same way, fear needs a doorway into your life. I am not afraid of dogs and I never have been. Why? Nothing has opened that door. If we deal with the event that gave fear its access to our lives, it is much easier to conquer. Not only that, maintaining the victory is almost effortless. Any time you recognize a fear in your life, ask the Lord to show you how it gained access.

After apologizing to the Lord for passing on fear to my daughter, I asked Him why I was an anxious passenger. Almost immediately, the Lord reminded me of an incident that had taken place 35 years earlier when I was just 15 years old. I had fallen asleep in the front seat of a car while a friend was driving me home from an event. We were traveling at about 70 miles an hour in the fast lane on the highway when I awoke to see us hurtling towards another vehicle.

"Jane!" I screamed. My cry woke the driver just in time for her to slam her foot on the brake, lessening the impact as we smashed into the other car. Miraculously, no other vehicles piled into ours and no-one was hurt. But I was terribly distressed. Not knowing how to process trauma, I tried to shake off the shock, then I buried the memory. The result: fear found a home in my heart and I was a nervous passenger for more than three decades. Not only that, I unwittingly passed that fear to my daughter. It's not just instinct that says that fear (as well as other emotional issues) can be passed down to the next generation, it's science. Epigenetics has shown that non-biological traits can be transmitted. My unresolved problems affected my daughter.

Dealing With Shock And Pain

When the Lord brought me back to that teenage crash, I dealt with the memory in prayer. Lamentations 2:19 says, "...Pour out your heart like water before the face of the Lord..." I poured out my heart before the Lord and told Him how afraid I felt. I shared the shock and horror of the accident, and He healed my heart. I then asked Him to fill me with His perfect peace. My prayers closed the door to fear.

The next time I was in the car, I glared at huge trucks in neighboring lanes, and quietly but sternly asserted, "I'm not scared!" I no longer tolerated any in-car nerves. I looked them in the face, dismantled any lies I believed, and calmed my heart. Driving became a much more enjoyable experience. My change enabled me to help my daughter to conquer her fears.

How Did Fear Find A Way In?

Slamming doors, screeching voices, and brutal beatings are terribly distressing. Car wrecks, agonizing procedures, bites, or attacks can be terrifying. All forms of trauma can open the door to fear. Then there is the fear of experiencing pain again. If you have been pushed away by someone you dearly loved, you may be afraid of rejection. If you were humiliated in front of a room full of people, you could be anxious about speaking in social settings. If you have been affected by chronic physical pain, you may be afraid of sickness. When you go through a harrowing experience, you may end up afraid of history repeating itself.

Let's look at the story of a woman told in 1 Samuel 25:2-3: "Now there was a man in Maon... The name of the man was Nabal, and the name of his wife Abigail. And she was a woman of good understanding and beautiful appearance; but the man was harsh and evil in his doings..." Abigail was a good woman but she was married to a harsh and crooked man. Being around someone who is harsh and angry can be terrifying. It's not just that harshness hurts, which it does. It's the unpredictability of anger.

Although God sometimes gets angry, His emotions are predictable. The Bible tells us what makes Him cross and we know that His displeasure will not last long. Psalms 30:5 says, "For His anger is but for a moment, His favor is for life..." What makes anger frightening is when it is unpredictable. Perhaps you have spent seasons of your life 'walking on eggshells' in your own home. You never knew what might cause your spouse to fly off the handle. Maybe your dad or mom was always angry so you tiptoed your way through life.

Later on in this account, we are told about a time when Abigail's staff asked her to handle a situation involving her husband. In 1 Samuel 25:17 (NLT), the people said, "You need to know this and figure out what to do, for there is going to be trouble for our master and his whole family. He's so ill-tempered that no-one can even talk to him!" You can hear the stress and apprehension in this conversation. Later on, we are also told that Nabal was a drunk.

Distress At Home

Maybe you have suffered the pain of a strained marriage. Perhaps you have lived with someone who constantly yelled or came home drunk. Addiction hurts everyone. Both the addict, and their nearest and dearest, get wounded by the destruction it causes. God's plan was that family would be a source of love, acceptance, and security. If your home felt like an unsafe place, fear will probably have found a way into your life. The Lord wants to heal you of the traumas you endured, and He longs to bring restoration into the depths of your heart.

Jonathan is another Bible character who suffered at the hands of his family. Let's look at 1 Samuel 20:30, 33 (NLT): "Saul boiled with rage at Jonathan. 'You stupid son of a whore!' he swore at him. 'Do you think I don't know that you want him to be king in your place, shaming yourself and your mother?' Then Saul hurled his spear at Jonathan, intending to kill him..." First, King Saul tore his son Jonathan apart with his words. He swore at him and insulted the young man's mother.

Words can cause deep wounds, especially when they are spoken by someone you love. Proverbs 12:18 says, "There is one who speaks like the piercings of a sword..." If you have been cut to the heart by something someone said, the Lord wants to heal your heart. The Bible says that cruel comments are life knife wounds in this verse. Just as a physical attack would be traumatic, so a verbal onslaught can cut you up on the inside. If you have been hurt by words, the Lord wants to remove the fiery dart from your soul and calm your heart. When you are healed of the hurts that opened the door to fear, it loses its power.

Sometimes fear is learned, as we already discovered. If your mother was a worrier, you may suffer from anxiety. If your father was always looking over his shoulder, you may be overly wary. Recognizing how fear entered is important so that you can firmly close the door. When it is passed down, you need to renounce the generational sin, then take authority over the spirit of fear and face it down.

2. Dismantling Fear's Power

Fear involves torment (1 John 4:18) which is severe mental or emotional distress. It is torment that makes fear frightening. It might be the thought of humiliating yourself in front of a room full of people, it could be the terror of dogs snapping, snakes hissing, or even blood. You may dread public speaking, social settings, or exams. Fear makes you turn away from the image that you dread. But fear loses its power when you remove the torment!

It starts with one simple step: in the presence of the Lord, face the sights that once caused dread. John 8:32 says, "And you shall know the truth, and the truth shall make you free." The Greek for know, 'ginōskō', means to be sure, to feel, to understand, and to perceive. This is not head knowledge. It is a deep inner assurance. When you know the truth about your situation, fear evaporates.

Let's use spiders as an example. If you are afraid of them, it is the fear of that insect that gives it power in your life. The truth is that virtually every spider is completely harmless. You are a towering giant in comparison. In the same way, people who have intimidated you are not all-powerful. They are mere mortals. Places where terrible things have happened are not sinister. You just need to be healed of what happened there. When you *know* the truth deep down, you will be free.

If you are afraid of rats, it is time to calmly picture one of those small furry creatures in prayer. Look confidently, knowing that the Lord is with you. If you were afraid of rejection, in prayer, picture yourself being pushed away and visualize the Lord holding you close. If there was someone that you were terrified of upsetting, imagine their face, smile at them in your heart, knowing that it doesn't matter if they are upset because God will never leave you.

Smashing Exam Jitters

Sasha, a lady from London, was due to sit some nursing exams. She was a smart woman who had studied, so she knew everything back to front. However, she kept failing and having to retake exams because fear paralyzed her each time she entered the examination hall. Desperate to graduate, she asked for my help. I led her in prayer. Once we had honored the presence of God, I asked her to visualize herself entering the huge test center, with her big brother Jesus at her side.

An exam room is not a frightening place unless you believe that to be the case. It is just a large hall filled with desks and chairs. In prayer, Sasha saw herself walk straight to her seat, knowing that she was not alone. Once at her desk, she looked around the large room, then I encouraged her to calmly declare, "I'm not afraid of this place. I'm not scared of the exam. I have the Lord with me, and I have the mind of Christ (see 1 Corinthians 2:16). I've got this and God's got me!"

We then rebuked the spirit of fear. This was simple now that Sasha had faced (and squashed!) her fears. We spent no more than a few minutes praying together. At the end of our call, peace reigned once again. Sasha called me a couple of weeks later to share the great news that she had passed her nursing exams with flying colors. Instead of turning away from fears, face them and dismantle the lies that held you captive. Only turn away when you are no longer intimidated.

The Power Of Painful Memories

Flashbacks are distressing, so the temptation is to hide from the rewind. Our memories end up becoming objects of dread and develop a power of their own to cause anguish. As a result, we shut away certain episodes in 'no-go' rooms hidden in our hearts. We dare not open the doors of those rooms because the contents are too painful. When something opens the door, we try to turn our faces away so that we don't have to feel the pain again. We think that by avoiding those recollections, we are protecting ourselves. The truth is that if you run away from distressing memories, they gain power through your fear.

Fear will tell you who or what to avoid, what to say, and how to think. Please don't give in. It may take time to conquer, but your freedom is worth the fight. Psalms 23:4 (TPT) says, "Lord, even when your path takes me through the valley of deepest darkness, fear will never conquer me, for you already have! You remain close to me and lead me through it all the way. Your authority is my strength and my peace. The comfort of Your love takes away my fear. I'll never be lonely, for You are near." Decide right now that you won't allow fear to control any area of your life any longer.

Don't Take Me Back There

Entering a random address into my GPS, I headed to a meeting with one of our leaders. Glancing up at the city signpost, I suddenly discovered I was back in the town where my daughter died a couple of months earlier. My heart raced and my palms sweated as I pulled over to calm my nerves. I did my best to suppress the unwelcome emotion before making my way again. I had intentionally avoided anything that brought me back to my pain.

It wasn't just towns and hospitals; I desperately tried to avoid remembering the last 24 hours of my daughter's life... I would see my little girl lying unwell on my tummy in the middle of the night, then I would remember my fear as she kept snuggling as close as she could. I would find myself back in that horrible place of panic, not knowing what to do. When I was unable to suck myself out of the memory cycle, they would continue...

I would see Naomi asleep the next morning as I went to work. I would see myself on the train to London, and I would hear that fraught phone call with my husband. Finally, I would receive that message: Naomi had been rushed to the hospital. These memories had the power to suck me into deep dread, so I would do everything to avoid these sights. I was tormented by my memories and anything that reminded me of that fateful day.

Those memories tormented me – that is, until the day I faced them a couple of months after our little one died. I couldn't cope with the power of these recollections any longer. Closing my eyes in prayer, I began to tell Jesus, my Wonderful Counsellor (see Isaiah 9:6), about the last 24 hours of my daughter's life. I shared every detail of those awful moments. I told Him about the horror, the anxiety, and the heartbreak. I told Him how helpless I felt watching while medics worked around the clock. One of my worst pictures was of Naomi being wrapped by a doctor in an aluminum sheet in an attempt to raise her body temperature. There were tubes pumping into her tiny frame. I poured out deep wells of pain in prayer, and the Lord started to heal my heart, one broken piece at a time. Not only that, the torment and dread left and never returned.

God does not want you to be afraid of revisiting any memory. Lamentations 3:20 describes how unhealed experiences feel: "My soul still remembers and sinks within me." If there is any event of the past that you can't think about without churning, the Lord wants to heal your heart. Lamentations 2:19a says, "...pour out your heart like water before the face of the Lord..." Set some time aside to tell your Heavenly Father what you have been through. When you go back to the pain in prayer, and talk to the Lord, you will begin a journey to restoration. Not only that, you will close fear's door.

3. Breaking Intimidation

Intimidation is fear's big brother. It is a bully that wants to squash you into submission. Intimidation fills its victims with dread. It tries to force you into fulfilling its demands. When you are intimidated, you feel threatened, your stomach churns, your heart is heavy, you may even be shaky. It is almost unbearable. 1 Corinthians 7:23 says, "You were bought at a price; do not become slaves of men." This enemy wants to make you its slave.

Although intimidation is channeled through people, it is important to remember the real identity of your enemy. Ephesians 6:12 (NIV) states, "Our struggle is not against flesh and blood, but against the rulers, against the authorities, against the powers of this dark world and against the spiritual forces of evil in the heavenly realms." People are not your problem. After you have conquered intimidation, you will be at peace in the company of those who once caused you to cower.

My Fight With Intimidation

My husband and I went through a dreadful season in ministry. It felt like we were on a rowing boat in the middle of a dark, stormy sea, being tossed about the wind and waves. I have never felt so shaken. After everything calmed down, I found myself suffering from anxiety. The slightest reminder of the season we had just left sent me into a spin. News items, passing references in conversations or any mention of the people involved would cause instant and intense emotional reactions. My peace would vanish, my stomach would knot up, while my heart rate would increase. Controlling my breathing only brought me momentary relief.

I tried taking authority over the spirit of intimidation and casting off my cares about the future, but that was only part of the problem. Shock and pain were trapped in my soul. I realized that I had been traumatized during that period. I could not get rid of the anxiety until the pain was healed. And I could not get rid of the pain until I went back to those memories. I got into God's presence and told my Heavenly Father exactly what had hurt me and how it made me feel. I shared the shock, the fear, and the pain with the Lord in as much detail as I could, and He healed my heart.

After the healing flowed, I was able to deal with the spirit of intimidation. It wasn't long before I was back to full strength. Words that once triggered anxiety now passed by unnoticed. Faces that had caused concern now provoked love. The way we know that we have been set free is that the memories that once triggered negative reactions lose their power. Does anyone intimidate you? It could be people in authority. It might be certain family members or people at your place of work. Perhaps you are intimidated by your spouse.

Before we go any further, ask the Lord to reveal the reason for your intimidation. Buried pain is often lurking beneath the surface when you are contending with this foul enemy. It's helpful to know for sure if old wounds gave fear access, so that we can firmly close the door by leading you into healing. We will deal with trapped pain in prayer at the end of this chapter. However, it's not always the past that attracts intimidation. If you have just stepped into a new dimension of influence, the enemy may use intimidation to try to prevent your promotion.

New Levels, New Devils

Paul (also known as Saul) was officially released into ministry by the disciples of Jesus. Acts 13:2-3 tells the story: "As they ministered to the Lord and fasted, the Holy Spirit said, 'Now separate to Me Barnabas and Saul for the work to which I have called them.' Then, having fasted and prayed, and laid hands on them, they sent them away." Immediately after Paul was officially released into ministry, the enemy opposed him.

Acts 13:8-10 says, "But Elymas the sorcerer (for so his name is translated) withstood them, seeking to turn the proconsul away from the faith. Then Saul, who also is called Paul, filled with the Holy Spirit, looked intently at him and said, 'O full of all deceit and all fraud, you son of the devil, you enemy of all righteousness, will you not cease perverting the straight ways of the Lord?'"

Intimidation always wants to turn people against you. It seeks to use disapproval to make you bow. The devil was not pleased that Paul had been promoted so he stirred up strife and fierce opposition. The Bible says that Elymas 'withstood' Paul. The word in Greek is 'anthistēmi' and it means to oppose. Elymas incited animosity against Paul. This could have been terribly intimidating. When you are about to step into something new, the devil wants you to be browbeaten and overcome with fear.

Paul responded decisively. He came back at the enemy with authority. He refused to be daunted and instead overpowered the spirit of intimidation. 2 Timothy 1:7 (AMP) is clear: "For God did not give us a spirit of timidity (of cowardice, of craven and cringing and fawning fear), but [He has given us a spirit] of power and of love and of calm and well-balanced mind and discipline and self-control." You have what it takes to defeat the spirit of intimidation. We will come back to this Scripture and take authority later in this chapter.

Words That Wound and Wind

Harsh words can tear you apart. Proverbs 12:18a says, "There is one who speaks like the piercings of a sword..." This Scripture compares cruel remarks with a stabbing. Just as a knife attack can be fatal, verbal abuse can choke its victims. It's not just what is said, but the way that insults are hurled that can be crippling. If you have been attacked with words, this could have opened the door to fear. Verbal attacks come in many guises, including insults, ridicule, twisted truth, cruelty, and even exposed secrets. Each of these can come with such force that they can create intimidation.

There is something about bullying, whether it is experienced by a child or an adult, that is particularly vicious. Bullying is when someone who has some sort of perceived or actual weakness is antagonized by another who has a form of strength. The 'weakness' could be age, size, seniority, isolation, or accent – the list is endless. Bullying is cowardly, it is cruel, and it can be mortifying. Bullying usually involves a mixture of harassment and humiliation which can strip its victims of any sense of dignity. It is shocking, and often leaves its victim cowering under intimidation.

The Bible calls Satan 'the accuser of the brethren' because accusation is one of the devil's most trusted tactics for damaging Christians. Accusation is a mix of judgement and vitriol, often laced with hatred. Full of blame, it can make its targets feel disqualified, and that can cause even a strong soul to throw in the towel. If you have been hurt and intimidated by accusation, the Lord wants to heal your heart and set you free.

David suffered many betrayals and accusations. In Psalms 55:2-5 (AMPC), he cried out to the Lord after a lifelong friend stabbed him in the back, "...I am restless and distraught in my complaint... [And I am distracted] at the noise of the enemy, because of the oppression and threats of the wicked; for they would cast trouble upon me, and in wrath they persecute me. My heart is grievously pained within me... Fear and trembling have come upon me;

horror and fright have overwhelmed me." David described the fear and pain that he felt during this season of his life. He told the Lord how he felt when he was betrayed by his former friend.

Remember that our struggle is never against flesh and blood (see Ephesians 6:12). People are not our real problem. This passage describes the effect that verbal attacks can have. Every word is troubling. They cause pain and often leave us trembling. Listen to the same passage in the New Living Translation: "I am overwhelmed by my troubles. My enemies shout at me, making loud and wicked threats. They bring trouble on me and angrily hunt me down. My heart pounds in my chest." (Psalms 55:2-4) This describes the state of someone who is gripped with fear, and not just pain.

4. Dealing With Fear's Triggers

Running into the arms of your Heavenly Father is not the only answer. We are instructed to deal with fear. Psalms 91:5-6 (NLT) says, "Do not be afraid of the terrors of the night, nor the arrow that flies in the day. Do not dread the disease that stalks in darkness, nor the disaster that strikes at midday." Perhaps if this was being written today, it would say: "Do not be afraid of the thumping footsteps behind you. Do not be afraid of being hated or humiliated. Do not dread cancer, heart attack, or any deadly virus. Do not fear accidents, crashes or disasters." God wants you to reach a place where nothing makes you afraid.

"Benjy has been hit by a car." Our babysitter continued, "He is OK, but he is in an ambulance on his way to hospital." My husband and I were at a conference when the call came. The hour's drive to my six-year-old son felt like forever as I imagined how he must be feeling. He had run ahead of his babysitter and out onto the road just as a car drove around the corner. Thrown over the hood and then back down onto the ground, he was cut and bruised, but had no obvious broken bones. Doctors were assessing him for any unseen injuries. I was in a mess until I reached the hospital and saw Benjy's sweet face. I could tell he would be fine.

Afterwards, I asked my husband about the incident, because I noticed that he remained calm through it all. "I bound the spirit of fear immediately and then started to declare God's Word over our son," Paul explained. His first response was prayer. While I was fearing the worst, my husband was in faith and believing for the best. I was terrified. Paul was trusting. I asked the Lord to teach me how to conquer fear. Although He did not orchestrate what happened next, He used it to show me the right way to respond...

A few months later, while my son was at a party, the mother of the birthday boy called me. "Jo, I'm so sorry..." I could hear panic in Catherine's voice. "Ben has been hit by a car! I think he is OK, but I'm so sorry..." This time, I chose to be calm. I asked some key questions to establish the facts and reassured the lady that everything would be well. I did not allow my thoughts to be dominated by anxiety. I instead focused on building my faith. More often than not, fear is a waste of energy which only makes difficult situations worse. I also did what I should have done earlier and taught my son about road safety!

Reign In Your Reactions

Fear is a controllable reflex. It might seem like alarm and horror are inevitable in terrible situations. However, once you know how to reign in your reactions, you will realize that fear can be a choice. John 14:1a (AMP) is crystal clear: "Do not let your hearts be troubled (distressed, agitated) ..." Another version puts it like this: "Don't worry or surrender to your fear..." This verse is straightforward. You and I must refuse distress and agitation, we must not surrender to fear.

On numerous occasions, the Bible instructs us not to be afraid. This is different to taking authority over fear once it has taken hold. You and I need to learn how to be at peace when the enemy is tempting us to fear. On at least 58 occasions, the Bible says, "... do not be afraid..." The New Testament alone commands us not to fear 27 times. Only twice in the New Testament are we instructed to resist or expel fear. Our first response to anxiety or dread needs to be a positive choice. I thank God for the chance to learn that lesson the second time Benjy was hit by a car. I have put this principle into practice many times since...

My husband's family has a history of heart disease. Paul's dad died of a heart attack in his early sixties, as did several of his uncles. One night, my husband suffered from severe palpitations which caused his heart to beat profusely. I could feel something like a soft golf ball pounding out of the side of his ribs. Fear tried to grip me. Jesus told a dad whose daughter was on the brink of death, "Do not be afraid, only believe." (Mark 5:36) Fear and faith are opposites; in order to have faith to pray in a crisis, we need to drive out fear.

Fear was my greatest enemy in that moment. I was afraid that my husband would die. I needed to take hold of my reactions and dismantle torment. The main threat I was hearing was the suggestion that I could not survive without my husband. So, I spoke back; my goal was to dismantle fear's power: "If my husband were to die, I would get healed by my faithful God. I would help my children to be healed. I would eventually come out the other side stronger than ever." Then the enemy reminded me that I was not good at managing finances, so I continued, "I would enlist the help of my son in all my financial affairs." I reined in my reactions, pulled apart the enemy's threats, and fear lost its victory. I then reminded myself of God's promises concerning healing. Faith arose and I prayed for my husband's health.

What Are Your Greatest Fears?

Jeremiah 42:11 says, "'Do not be afraid of the king of Babylon, of whom you are afraid; do not be afraid of him,' says the Lord, 'for I am with you, to save you and deliver you from his hand.'"

The king of Babylon was probably the most powerful man on earth at that time. Without divine intervention, he could have destroyed the Israelites. God does not want you to remain afraid of anything. In essence, that verse is saying: do not be afraid of your greatest fear!

Look at the threats that Satan is waving in front of your face, grab them out of his hand and then tear them into tiny pieces. See your fears from a heavenly perspective. They are nothing before the face of the Lord. Don't be afraid of the devil's worst weapons. Even death has been defeated by the resurrection of Jesus. If the enemy tries to make you anxious, boldly declare, "O death, where is your victory? O death, where is your sting?" (Corinthians 15:55 NLT) If you refuse to be afraid of harm or even death, the devil will find it much harder to torment you.

It was about five years before my dad passed away that I realized I was not ready for him die. We had experienced a fright over his health which drew the issue to my attention. I decided to deal with it in prayer. Hebrews 9:27b (NLT) says, "...each person is destined to die once..." Death is inevitable. Although we never want anyone to go before their time, we need to settle the mortality of our loved ones in our hearts. I allocated some time to pray about my dad's life. I acknowledged that he would pass away one day. I faced the fact that his life had an expiration date and asked the Lord to prepare me for his death. I was no longer afraid, and although I needed healing when he passed away, there was no shock and the Lord restored me supernaturally quickly.

I am not afraid of my mom's passing, my passing, or the passing of anyone I love. Dreading death gives the devil power in our lives. When we get a heavenly perspective, we realize that the end of our days on earth represents graduation to glory. Jesus came to break the bondage of fear of death. Hebrews 2:15 (AMP) says, "And also that He might deliver and completely set free all those who through the [haunting] fear of death were held in bondage throughout the whole course of their lives." It's time to enjoy the freedom Christ has provided.

Catch That Thought

When an anxious idea disturbs you, don't allow it to find a home. Be conscious of what you are meditating on and be quick to catch negativity. Colossians 3:2 (MSG) says, "Don't shuffle along, eyes to the ground, absorbed with the things right in front of you. Look up, and be alert to what is going on around Christ—that's where the action is. See things from His perspective." God is bigger than the things that are bigger than you. He is your Defender. Don't allow the devil to decide what you dwell on. Instead, become deliberate about choosing your perspective. You can steer your thoughts in the right direction by refusing to dwell on anything you dread, and focus on the greatness of God.

Fear is rooted in deception. Sometimes the threats that the enemy whispers in our ears are a complete fabrication. For example, fear will make you believe that a common spider is a terrible threat. It will tell you that you can never get into a car again after that crash. It will try to convince you that the examination is too difficult. By pedaling lies like these, the devil makes you think that the challenge that you are facing is overwhelming. Fear will magnify any problem. When we separate falsehood from fear, it becomes easier to tackle and defeat.

Even when there is some factual basis for what fear says, it is still propelled by deception. For example, there is only a tiny chance that the car on the other side of the road will hit your vehicle. The call from your child's school is highly unlikely to be tragic news. You probably will succeed in that exam or business venture. Even if it does not work out the way you want, Jesus will never forsake you. 2 Corinthians 10:5b says, "...bringing every thought into captivity to the obedience of Christ." Choose to catch fearful sentiments before they settle in your soul and try to take root. Silence Satan's threats by reminding yourself of the faithfulness of your Heavenly Father. Confront fear's lies with the truth in God's Word. Rein in your reactions and you will enjoy a new freedom.

5. Know Your Strength

When Jesus went to the cross, He gave you the authority that belongs to Him. You are an overcomer, but you need to take what is yours. 2 Timothy 1:7 (AMP) says, "For God did not give us a spirit of timidity (of cowardice, of craven and cringing and fawning fear), but [He has given us a spirit] of power and of love and of calm and well-balanced mind and discipline and self-control." If we will use the power He has given us, choose love, and align our thoughts with His, we will conquer fear. You don't need to be anxious. You don't need to be intimidated. You don't need to worry what people think. This verse gives us three weapons that we can use to obliterate fear.

Your Three-Pronged Authority

Power is given to every believer when they make Jesus Lord. When Jesus released the great commission, He told the disciples that they had authority over the enemy. Luke 10:19 (AMP) says, "Behold! I have given you authority and power to trample upon serpents and scorpions, and [physical and mental strength and ability] over all the power that the enemy [possesses]; and nothing shall in any way harm you." You can trample the enemy under your feet. None of his plots against you will harm you. That's the truth.

For more than thirty years, I was wary of a particular lady. I would avoid seeing her or speaking to her too often. She had caused pain in the past, so I saw avoidance as a wise way of protecting myself. During a difficult season, I was forced to obliterate the power of intimidation over my life. It was not a quick fix, but after three or four rounds with the devil in the boxing ring, I won! It was around this time that a mutual friend was talking to this woman on the phone. To my surprise, I chipped in, "Let me say hello!" My friend passed me the phone and I enjoyed a short conversation with this lady.

Later that day, I reflected on that moment and realized that I had been afraid of that woman for years. Because I had been overcoming intimidation in other areas of my life, a previously invisible fear had evaporated. I began to understand the verse that says, "There is no fear in love; but perfect love casts out fear... But he who fears has not been made perfect in love." (1 John 4:18) I had often wondered why the Bible said that love casts out fear when I was certain that fear could only be driven out by prayer in the name of Jesus. I also could not understand why being fearful could make me less loving until God showed me.

Who Is At The Center?

Fear of being hurt usually has self-interest at the center. It makes you feel like a victim and causes you to protect yourself. It makes you afraid of the pain or problems that another person may cause. Love, in contrast, is otherly. When fear says, "You could hurt me," love says, "I could help you." When fear seeks to guard self, love seeks to do good for someone else. Fear is incompatible with love. This is especially true when it comes to fear of people's opinions. If I am intimidated by a relative or friend, I will be concerned about how they could hurt me. I might be uneasy about speaking up in case I am made to feel small.

Fear of man is clearly self-centered, but it is also evident in other arenas. The fear I felt as a passenger was focused on me. I was not overly concerned about my driver or the well-being of people in other vehicles. Someone who is afraid of spiders is rarely thinking about the impact that an insect might have on others. Even if you're afraid for someone you love, concern for people in the wider community is not normally at the forefront of your mind. In truth, the more we love others, the less space we will have for fear.

Let's look at 1 John 4:18a (AMP): "There is no fear in love [dread does not exist], but full-grown (complete, perfect) love turns fear out of doors and expels every trace of terror..." When we are filled with the love of God, fear gets driven out. When we move our thoughts from self to someone else, we will be expelling intimidation. I had not just been 'wary' of the lady that I mentioned at the start of this section. For years I had been afraid of her hurting me. When fear of that woman left, love for her filled my heart and I was able to minster comfort and strength.

Love makes you victorious because love never fails (see 1 Corinthians 13:8). Next time you are afraid, draw near to God. Take your eyes off the object of your fear and shift your focus to your Heavenly Father. Ask the Lord to fill you with His love. It will make you a powerful force in God's kingdom.

Clear and Calm

Fear clouds good judgement and sensible decisions. It causes us to lose our peace and prevents logical thinking. When you are free from fear, you are able to judge what is right and best. You will be able to make good choices and you can think clearly. Let's look again at what 1 Timothy 1:7b (AMP) says. "…[He has given us a spirit] of power and of love and of calm and well-balanced mind and discipline and self-control." Jesus has paid the price for you to have a calm inner atmosphere. Just as you need to rise up and take your authority, so you also need to protect your peace.

Fear tries to force a reaction, whereas we have been given self-control and discipline. Next time fear tries to influence your thinking, take charge of your thoughts and remind yourself that the Prince of Peace is the Lord of your life. Isaiah 26:3a (AMP) says, "You will guard him and keep him in perfect and constant peace whose mind is stayed on You…" You are the boss of your inner atmosphere. You choose what you allow to dominate. When you pull your thoughts back to the safety of your Heavenly Father, and remind yourself that you are a conqueror, agitation and anxiety will evaporate.

The Lord is not only in your corner, He made the way for your peace. Isaiah 53:5 (NIV) says: "But He was pierced for our transgressions, He was crushed for our iniquities; the punishment that brought us peace was on Him, and by His wounds we are healed." Jesus was crushed for your sake. He suffered so that you could enjoy perfect peace. Although fear is your enemy, it is vital that you lower your opinion of its power. Fear wants to control you, but when you recognize that you are the boss, you will be able to put it in its rightful place. Just like the battles we have with sin and sickness, I think that you and I will probably have to fight fear until we graduate to glory. But every conquest makes us stronger.

6. Take Your Authority

Jesus disarmed Satan's power publicly (see Colossians 2:15). He has removed the 'sting from the scorpion' so all you and I need to do is execute our rights. Fear is a spirit. In Luke 10:19, Jesus said, "Behold, I give you the authority to trample on serpents and scorpions, and over all the power of the enemy, and nothing shall by any means hurt you." Jesus has given you authority over all the power of the enemy, and of course that includes fear and intimidation. It is time to take advantage of the upper hand that God has given you.

James 4:7 explains how you can employ your spiritual authority: "Therefore submit to God. Resist the devil and he will flee from you." There are three parts to this verse. Our authority over the enemy comes from being under the authority of the Most High God. First, we need to submit. That means that we need to surrender afresh to Jesus. When we are afraid, we have taken our eyes off the Lord, and we have given our attention to the enemy's threats. In essence, we have stopped trusting.

The day I realized that fear is a sin was liberating. It helped me to develop a zero-tolerance attitude. Romans 14:23 says, "But he who doubts is condemned… for whatever is not from faith is sin." I encourage you to accept responsibility for allowing fear to find a home in your heart. Say sorry to God for being afraid instead of trusting. This is an important part of submitting to the Lordship of Christ.

The Days Of Living In Fear Are Over

Secondly, we need to resist the devil. We need to renounce our relationship with fear and make a determined decision that we will no longer tolerate its influence in our lives. This does not mean that we will no longer have to contend with this enemy. It means that we have declared war and will no longer take it lying down. In Psalms 104:9, we read how God drew clear boundaries for the sea when He created the earth: "You have set a boundary that they may not pass over, that they may not return to cover the earth." That's what we do when we renounce fear. We say, "This far, but no further, in Jesus' name!"

Let's look again at Luke 10:19, where Jesus said, "Behold, I give you the authority to trample on serpents and scorpions, and over all the power of the enemy, and nothing shall by any means hurt you." He has given you authority over this foul spirit. You have the upper hand, and you can drive it out of your life. In fact, once you know how to rebuke this spirit, it will probably become a fairly regular habit. When I decided it was time to overcome the fear of horses, I rebuked the spirit then ran into a field full of the beautiful creatures. Any time it tries to creep up on me, I deal with my thoughts, confront any lies, and take authority.

James 4:7 ends by saying that the devil will flee. It's time to enjoy watching the enemy scarper. You don't need to tolerate this foul foe anymore. Proverbs 1:33 (NLT) says: "But all who listen to me will live in peace, untroubled by fear of harm." Perfect peace is your portion. I am going to lead you in prayer through each area we covered. Please don't skip past any of this, because you never know where your freedom will come from.

Heavenly Father,

I want to be completely free from every fear so that I can fulfill my destiny. Lord, I ask that You would reveal every hidden hurt or old wound that opened the door to fear. I invite Your searching gaze into my heart. Examine me through and through; find out everything that may be hidden within me. Sift through all my anxieties and reveal the things that allowed fear into my life.

Heal Me, Oh Lord

(As the Lord reveals painful memories, buried trauma, wounding words, or other hurtful experiences, tell Him exactly what you went through. Share how you felt in that moment. Explain why it hurt you so much. Pour out your heart like water before the face of the Lord. Know that He loves you and He wants to hear what you went through so that He can heal your precious heart.)

Please heal my heart, Oh Lord, I pray. In every place where there was once pain, I ask that You would fill me with Your healing love. Restore the depths of my soul as I remain in Your presence. I receive Your wonderful love; I am so grateful to be Your precious child. Because You freely forgive me, I choose to freely forgive those who have hurt me. I let them go. I don't want them to pay or suffer in any way. I release them and I ask You to bless them and their loved ones.

Dismantling Fear's Power

Lord, I am ready to dismantle fear's power. With You by my side, I calmly look at the object that once filled me with dread. (*Now tell the Lord what you are seeing. Dismantle any lies or threats. Look at the sight, then calmly and confidently say*) "You don't scare me. I am not afraid because Jesus is by my side." I take back control over my life, I won't listen to Satan's lies any longer.

I no longer fear what people think because I know what You think. I take my eyes off the faces of people and I look to Your affirming face, my Lord. I will no longer seek to please people because I desire to please You, Lord. I break the fear of man from my life in Jesus' name.

Breaking Intimidation

I refuse to be intimidated because the God of heaven and earth is with me. (*Picture the face of anyone that you find intimidating*) I look calmly at the face of the person that once frightened me. I declare that you are not God! You are a mere mortal. You are only human and I no longer allow fear of you to control my life. I fear God alone, I do not fear any human being. (*If that person has hurt you in any way, you need to forgive.*) I forgive you for hurting me, I forgive you for making me afraid. I release you; you don't owe me anything. I let you go. And Father, I ask that you would bless that person and their loved ones.

Reigning In My Reactions

From today, I will take captive every fearful thought. I will not allow my heart to be troubled, I will not surrender to any fears. I will choose how I respond to bad news, troubling times, sickness, unexpected bills and more, from this day forth. Holy Spirit, I ask You to remind me of my power over fear any time the enemy tries to make me afraid.

My Threefold Strength

Thank You, Lord, that You have not given me the spirit of fear. I declare that I have been empowered by the Spirit of God, I am bold, and I am strong because the Lord God is with me! I declare that the love of the Lord has been poured out in my heart. I am full of Your love, Heavenly Father. I will no longer be obsessed with protecting myself. Instead, I will clothe myself with Your loving kindness. Thank You, Lord, that my memory is blessed, thank You that I have the mind of Christ, and thank You that I have calm and well-balanced thoughts.

Taking Authority

I submit my whole life to You afresh, Jesus, You are my Lord. I apologize, Lord, for tolerating fear when fear is sin; I ask for Your forgiveness. I renounce fear from this day forth, I will no longer tolerate it in my life. I take authority over the spirit of fear, I bind the spirit of fear and intimidation, and in the name of Jesus, I drive it out of my life!

Father, I thank You that I am free from fear. I commit to conquer this enemy any time it tries to attack. I give You all the praise and glory for my newfound freedom!

In Jesus' precious name I pray,

Amen.

Chapter Seven

THE DESTINY TRAP

Imagine spending three years of your life with Jesus (here on earth). In that time, you would witness Him heal the sick, raise dead children to life, and walk on the sea in the middle of the night. Chosen to be part of His inner circle, you would be personally mentored by the Son of God. Any time you didn't understand something, you could ask the Lord. You would see Jesus speak to raging storms and watch the winds instantly cease. You would witness Him cast demons out of a madman who was immediately restored to his right mind. You would see entire cities impacted by the love and miracles of the Messiah.

That was the life that Judas lived. Despite all that he had experienced over the course of three mind-blowing years, Judas became offended, turned against Jesus, and lost everything. Notice that when Jesus chose Judas to be one of His disciples, he had a good heart. In listing the twelve, Luke 6:16b says, "...and Judas Iscariot who also became a traitor." So he was not a traitor when he first joined the team. Instead of seeing Judas as *the enemy*, let's recognize that he was human. If it could happen to one of Jesus' closest companions, it could happen to you, it could happen to me. Instead of assuming you are immune to offense, please ask the Holy Spirit to reveal any issues hiding in your heart. Ask the Lord to teach you how to protect yourself. Let's pray before we go any further.

Heavenly Father,

I humble myself before You today. Please will You search my heart and reveal any hidden offenses. Please expose any attitudes that make me prone to offense. Cleanse my soul and purify my thoughts so that I can please you and fulfill my destiny.

In Jesus' name I pray,

Amen.

The gospels tell the story of a woman who poured an entire bottle of sweet-smelling oil over Jesus' feet. John 12:5 reports that Judas made the following resentful statement: "Why was this fragrant oil not sold for three hundred denarii and given to the poor?" His comment must have been loud enough for nearby people to hear, because a group of onlookers soon repeated his criticism. Mark 14:4-5 explains, "But there were some who were indignant among themselves, and said, 'Why was this fragrant oil wasted? For it might have been sold for more than three hundred denarii and given to the poor.' And they criticized her sharply." Any time I criticize a brother or sister, my words sow seeds into the hearts of those listening. My negativity can, and will, infect other people's opinions. Made in the image of God, we all have the power to influence. We choose whether we use that privilege to promote love or cause division.

I believe that Judas's words infected a group of bystanders. Their conversation in turn justified Judas in his offense. Mark 14:10 says, "Then Judas Iscariot, one of the twelve, went to the chief priests to betray Him to them." This verse starts with the word, *Then,* which firmly links it with the preceding verses. Offense breeds offense in others, so we must uproot it from our hearts to protect ourselves, and others. Offense caused Judas to offer his help to the religious leaders who wanted to destroy Jesus. When we are offended, our hearts harden. Romans 9:33 speaks about a "rock of offense" because an offense is like a rock in your soul. Unfortunately, hardness is a serious issue. It causes us to put our fingers in our ears. It makes us insensitive to conviction and it causes us to refuse correction. I have seen offended people throw away destiny relationships, change jobs, leave churches, and even emigrate. Offense is a destiny destroying heart issue.

Almost Incurable

Not only is it dangerous, offense is difficult to cure. Proverbs 18:19 says, "A brother offended is harder to win than a strong city..." I have never tried to overthrow a city, but I imagine it would take an immensely clever plan and a powerful army! The Bible tells us that conquering a city is easier than trying to win back the heart of someone who is offended. Please allow that truth to sink deep down in your soul. If offense is common (which it is), that means that you will have to deal with offense in your own life. And if it is that difficult to help the offended, then you need to know how to be watchful over your own heart.

If you challenge a brother or sister about offense, they will usually tell you that you are wrong and defend themselves, "I'm not offended!" They will justify their attitudes, words or actions. They will build a wall around their hearts and keep you out. So, I have three suggestions that will help you to protect your destiny. Firstly, ask the Lord to show you any time your heart is hardening. Secondly, if you are not discerning the promptings of the Holy Spirit, ask Him to send someone to let you know that you are offended. Thirdly, make a decision before the Lord today that if *anyone, ever* tells you that you are offended, you will assume that their challenge is an answer to your prayer today. However much you want to defend yourself, resist. Instead, keep quiet, and make time to pray at your earliest opportunity.

When you pray, start by humbling yourself in the presence of God, repent of any pride or judgement arising inside, and ask the Holy Spirit to shine His light into your heart and reveal *any* hidden anger or upset. If you realize your heart has become hard, be quick to apologize to the Lord and to forgive anyone who has wronged you. You could come back to this very chapter. Read, re-read, and repent until your heart is soft like clay in the hands of the Lord. Let's pray now. This prayer could save your destiny.

Heavenly Father,

I humble myself in Your presence. I desire with all of my heart to fulfill Your plans and purposes for my life. I want to hear the words, "Well done, good and faithful servant," when I depart this mortal body. So, I ask You to protect me from becoming offended with anyone. I ask You to make me sensitive to my heart hardening. Help me to recognize when the actions, words, or attitudes of others are upsetting or annoying me. Help me to realize when I am becoming (even slightly) indignant towards the people around me.

If I am unable to hear the conviction of Your Spirit, Lord, I ask You to send someone to tell me that I am offended or that I need to forgive. I make a commitment to You today, for the sake of my destiny, that if anyone ever suggests that I might be offended or that I need to forgive, I will listen. I will not defend myself or suggest that they are mistaken. Instead, I will come to You in prayer. I will humble myself before You, and I will ask You to search my heart. I will ask You to expose any wrong within. I will forgive, even if I am not aware that I am holding unforgiveness. I will let go of upset, even if I feel justified. I will surrender my heart and life to You afresh. This is my commitment to You, Lord.

In Jesus' name I pray,

Amen.

Judas was present at the last supper when Jesus gave this warning: "Assuredly, I say to you, one of you who eats with Me will betray Me." (Mark 14:18) But Judas would not listen. His heart was hard. Offense is one of the devil's most trusted weapons to separate God's people from their destinies. It is also blinding. It blinds us to the truth. We dig in our heels and hold fast to our argument. We refuse to see any other perspective, but instead become all the more certain that we are right, and they are wrong.

Judas's weakness was money. Very often, when we have an issue, we see that problem everywhere we look. If you struggle with jealousy, you may wrongly assume others are envious. If you battle with lust, you may think everyone else does too. Because Judas was motivated by money, he did not like it when a woman poured an expensive oil over the feet of Jesus. He was offended at the Lord for accepting the extravagant offering. He didn't like the apparent wastage. The heart is deceitful so he will have believed his own interpretations, but deep down, Judas was jealous, and he was offended. Offense caused a man that once called Jesus his Lord to send him to his death.

What Is Offense?

The Greek for offense is 'skandalizō' and it means to entrap, to entice into sin, or to stumble. Our word scandalized is derived from skandalizō. The word originated from a term that describes the bait that is placed in a trap to entice prey. It is important to understand that the devil will try to entice us into offense until the day we die. Satan is a strategist. He devises plans to cause God's children to stumble. Numbers 25:18 says, "...they harassed you with their schemes by which they seduced you..." Offense is seductive, because taking the bait feels good to the flesh.

Let's look at how the devil devises a plan for your downfall. He will tempt you over time to bury small offenses against someone who is important to your purpose. Perhaps you know that being offended is wrong, so when that brother or sister does something that you do not like, you get past it and move on. You focus on the positives and ignore the irritation. But every time you sidestep an offense, it gets hidden in your soul. Mark 11:25 is clear: "And whenever you stand praying, if you have anything against anyone, forgive him, that your Father in heaven may also forgive you your trespasses."

Did you catch that? If you have *anything* against *anyone*, forgive them. Any time you are upset with someone, you need to forgive, however insignificant the issue. Forgive in Greek is 'aphiēmi', which means to send away or let go. When we forgive, we surrender every upset. Afterwards, we have *nothing* against that person and our hearts are pure and tender. If you don't release an upset, it will get buried in your heart. It will then just be a matter of time before the buildup of small offenses is sufficient to cause relationship breakdown. All it takes is a season when you are vulnerable mixed with a 'final straw'.

Strong's Bible dictionary unpacks the meaning further. It explains that offense causes a person *to distrust and desert one whom he ought to trust and even obey.* The very definition states that offense is often directed towards someone in authority. More often than not, the enemy tempts you to become offended with a person who is charged with helping you into your destiny. It plays out something like this... You see something that you dislike in someone who is in a position of authority in your life. This causes you to disapprove of that person and prevents you from acknowledging that person's authority. As a result, offense causes people to despise the very leaders charged with helping them to fulfill their purpose. Offense is a foul, demonic plot to separate God's people from their destinies by causing strategic rifts.

Let me also explain the difference between hurt and offense. When you are hurt, you are wounded, and you need healing. When you are offended, you may be hurt or upset, but you also feel angry or annoyed. If you are offended by something someone has done, you will want to shut them or their influence out. When you picture the person's face, you will feel some animosity.

How It Unfolds

It starts with a thought. The initial thought is not the offense – it is what you do with the thought. By rehearsing what you saw or heard, you start to be disturbed. You focus on the issue that upset you. You recount what you wish you had said or what you think they should have done. Indignation builds, and the unchecked thought grows into an offense. You feel like you have the right to be upset. Offense normally comes from four directions. It is caused by what people say: cruel comments or rude remarks. And by what they do not say: no-one thanks you for your labor of love, or your pastor fails to notice your hard work behind the scenes. Then it is prompted by what people do: someone takes your space in the parking lot or pushes past you to get the last available seat. You can become offended by what a person does or doesn't do: no-one calls when you are grieving, your leaders do not visit when they said they would, or your family forgets your child's birthday.

We all make mistakes and unknowingly hurt one another. You will have done or said things that could have caused offense. Knowing that might help you to overlook the things that could cause you to become upset. Loving others helps to keep us from offense. 1 Peter 4:8 (NLT) says, "Most important of all, continue to show deep love for each other, for love covers a multitude of sins." Having said that, another way to avoid offense is to stay on your healing journey. The more we are healed, the less we are likely to hold grudges due to the words or actions of others.

Who Does He Think He Is?

Have you ever felt irritated by the way someone was talking or behaving? It might be a co-worker or a family member. It could be someone in church or a preacher. Something rises inside as a result of the way they are carrying themselves. A group of people in Jesus' day felt the same way. They grew up with Jesus and knew Him personally. They didn't like the way He was acting. Matthew 13:55-57 describes their reaction: "'Is this not the carpenter's son? Is not His mother called Mary? And His brothers James, Joses, Simon, and Judas? And His sisters, are they not all with us? Where then did this Man get all these things?' So they were offended at Him..."

They didn't like seeing someone they knew rise high. Perhaps it made them feel inferior because their lives had not changed.

Whatever the reason, Jesus' newfound fame irritated them. How do you feel when someone you once considered a peer becomes successful? How do you react when co-workers get promoted over you? The enemy wants you to be upset by the opportunities enjoyed by others. He wants you to harden inside.

The Devil's Plan

The Parable of the Sower in Mark 4:16-17 (AMP) explains the purpose of offense: "The ones sown upon stony ground are those who... have no real root in themselves, and so they endure for a little while; then when trouble or persecution arises on account of the Word, they immediately are offended (become displeased, indignant, resentful) and they stumble and fall away." Offense steals the word from your heart. It makes you stumble and fall away. People have forsaken friends, left churches, taken their children out of their destinies, quit jobs, and resigned from positions – all because they were offended.

You might be thinking, "Well why not? If you aren't happy, then move on!" That might sound convincing, but Romans 8:14 says that the sons of God are led by the Spirit of God, not by offense. Every time you are wounded, you need to get healed and forgive, *then* ask God to reveal His will. If God tells you to move on, you can do it the right way: showing love and kindness to the people who hurt you.

Many years ago, we went through a painful season at church. A couple who had been in leadership for many years made a host of accusations against my husband and me. About a third of our congregation left. For a while, it seemed like everyone thought they could accuse us of anything. I was battered by the betrayal and offended at the way we had been treated. A couple of months after it all happened, my family went away for a few days to rest. One evening after the children had gone to bed, my husband asked me how I was doing. I remember my reply. "I feel like I've been marched onto the platform in our auditorium and stripped in front of everyone." I felt crushed and did not want to lead anymore. I loved Jesus, but I no longer liked the church.

Healing Is Not An Option

My husband listened lovingly and then responded. "I am giving you three weeks to get healed. Our church needs a healthy mother." As soon as we returned home, I got into the presence of God and poured out my pain. I told Him how much the words and actions of our people had hurt me. The Lord restored my heart, and I forgave anyone who had wounded us. That's when the Lord showed me that it is impossible to love the Lord and hate the church. Jesus is the head, but the church is *His* body. Any time I am angry with a Christian brother or sister, I am angry with one of God's children. 1 John 4:20 (NLT) says, "If someone says, 'I love God,' but hates a fellow believer, that person is a liar; for if we don't love people we can see, how can we love God, whom we cannot see?" Once I was healed, it was much easier to deal with offenses. I am so glad that my husband insisted on me getting restored. Some who had left returned, and I was able to welcome them back with open arms.

Offense is a test which you will have to pass again and again if you are going to fulfill your destiny. You might say that you are just angry or upset, but in truth, you are probably offended. Let me repeat again how to work out if you are hurt or if you are hurt *and* offended. When you consider the people who wronged you, how do you feel? If seeing their face in your mind's eye makes you irritated, then you are probably not just hurt, but also offended. If your hurt is mixed with a sense of injustice, then you are probably offended.

Proverbs 14:10 says, "The heart knows its own bitterness..." Deep down, if we will admit it, we know when our hearts have grown hard towards particular people. That's a sure sign that we are offended. Remember our prayer at the start of this chapter: if ever anyone tells you that you are offended, don't dismiss their suggestion, assume that they are telling the truth.

Could You Capture A City?

Let's look again at the extraordinary statement in Proverbs 18:19: "A brother offended is harder to win than a strong city..." I cannot imagine what it would take to overthrow a city! I am certain that I do not have the necessary skills. Yet the Bible tells us that it is even harder to win over someone who is offended. Anger at perceived injustice often makes us hold tight to our position. We must guard against this destiny destroyer. We need to learn to spot it in our own hearts, and we need to know how to expel it from our lives.

Offense incubates pride (that sense of superiority and judgment), and pride breeds offense. When we feel wronged, we often harden our hearts. Others may try to offer correction, but in that moment of indignation, we think they have no right. So, we have to learn to humble ourselves and accept correction. The truth is that we will all probably get offended from time to time. We need to be ready to spot faults in our own lives. It is a wonderful opportunity to kick pride out of our lives.

What Does God Think?

You might be saying that you are not easily offended. I have heard many people make that statement! Can I suggest that you ask the Holy Spirit for His opinion on that? According to the Bible, our hearts can (and do) lie to us. It is easier to believe our view of ourselves than the truth, because the truth is not always pretty. We do not know what is lurking inside. However, the Lord knows you and me better than we know ourselves. "The heart is deceitful above all things... Who can know it [perceive, understand, be acquainted with his own heart and mind]? I the Lord search the mind, I try the heart…" (Jeremiah 17:9-10 AMP)

On the night He was betrayed, Jesus predicted that Peter would deny Him. As one of His strongest leaders, Peter was adamant that he would remain faithful. Matthew 26:33 (AMP) says, "Peter declared to Him, 'Though they all are offended and stumble and fall away because of You [and distrust and desert You], I will never do so.'" Like many of us, the Apostle Peter thought that he was offense-proof, but he was dreadfully wrong.

Even if you are rarely offended, there is one type of person that can offend even those who are almost unoffendable! Proverbs 23:17 in the Passion Translation says, "Don't allow the actions of evil men to cause you to burn with anger…" One group of people who can easily cause loving people to get offended are those who are easily offended themselves. Guard yourself from becoming offended at offended people. Another Scripture that makes this point is Proverbs 24:19: "Don't be angrily offended over evil-doers or be agitated by them." (TPT) Let's make sure that we show patience and kindness to those who are throwing one accusation after another. We need to be extra vigilant to protect our hearts when we are around people who push our buttons. Love and forgiveness are the opposite to offense so, as Colossians 3:14 instructs, "…put on love, which is the bond of perfection."

You Never Know

I often think back to the day our two-year-old daughter died. We drove back from the hospital in a daze. We travelled slowly in the fast lane. The driver behind us became very annoyed, beeping and flashing his lights at us. We moved out of his way. It taught me an important lesson. You never know what someone else is going through. Sometimes the way people are behaving is nothing to do with you or me and everything to do with their own difficult journey. Let's try to remember that.

If someone hurts your feelings, mistreats you, or gets in your way, why not make a decision to be gracious and kind? It is amazing how much more enjoyable life is when we overlook the mistakes people make and give them the benefit of the doubt. Copy Jesus, who said, "I remember your sins no more." (Hebrews 8:12) Let the offense go and put on love. If a neighbor does something that bothers you, overlook it for love's sake and be kind to them in return.

Proverbs 19:11 says, "The discretion of a man makes him slow to anger and his glory is to overlook a transgression." It is glorifying to God when we overlook being wronged. A great way to avoid becoming offended is to become 'otherly'. When we keep our eyes off ourselves and consider the needs or feelings of others, it protects our hearts. Dealing with this foul destiny blocker is not easy, but it is essential.

How Could You?

Offense blames. You could hold someone responsible for your pain. Maybe you've walked through a really tough time, and no-one bothered to call. Perhaps leaders were insensitive, or friends didn't care. The problem is that when you blame, you deepen the invisible trenches around you and make your pain worse. When you blame others for part – or even all – of your misery, you relinquish control of your own happiness. You give others the keys to your wellbeing. Blame is pointless and it is destructive.

Let's look at what goes on inside when we blame someone. We are usually irritated or angry because we feel wronged. Our eyes are on the errors of others. Blame is usually rooted in judgement, which we know is dangerous. When we judge, it injures us more than those we hold responsible. Remember what Matthew 7:1-2 (AMPC) says: "Do not judge and criticize and condemn others... For just as you judge and criticize and condemn others, you will be judged and criticized and condemned, and in accordance with the measure you [use to] deal out to others, it will be dealt out again to you."

When I judge someone for the way they treat me, I open the door for others to criticize me when I get it wrong. Blame also stirs anger and frustration. Since the start of time, man has used blame to resist conviction. Adam's first instinct was to blame God and Eve when he was confronted about his sin.

Let's look at Genesis 3:12: "Then the man said, 'The woman whom You gave to be with me, she gave me of the tree, and I ate.'" Adam blamed God for giving him Eve. Then he blamed his wife for giving him the forbidden fruit. You can almost hear the sentiment behind his words. "It's not fair. I didn't ask for a woman. I didn't choose her. It's not my fault. I'm just a victim stuck in the middle." I wonder whether history may have told a different story if Adam had accepted responsibility for his mistakes? Blame got him nowhere.

You may not have done anything for which you need to take responsibility. You could be the victim of horrific circumstances. Irrespective of our innocence, we have a choice about whether we point the finger. 1 Peter 4:8 (AMPC) says, "...Love covers a multitude of sins [forgives and disregards the offenses of others]." Blame rehearses the wrongs of others. Love overlooks them. The latter might sound difficult, but it helps us on the road to recovery. We set ourselves free from the very people we were holding responsible.

Escalating Conversations

We have seen that offense blames, but it also talks. Matthew 12:34b says, "...out of the abundance of the heart the mouth speaks." When you are offended, you will find yourself talking about what happened whenever you get the chance. Proverbs 17:9 (AMP) says, "He who covers and forgives an offense seeks love, but he who repeats or harps on a matter separates even close friends." Offense is always looking to sow disunity. Proverbs 26:22 (AMP) says, "The words of a whisperer or slanderer are like dainty morsels or words of sport [to some, but to others are like deadly wounds]; and they go down into the innermost parts of the body [or of the victim's nature]." Sharing an offense feels good to the flesh, but it can cause both the speaker and their listeners to become infected.

Years ago, a man gave a brother some unwanted advice about a highly sensitive matter. My brother was outraged. I was a bit wary of the gentleman in question, so when the brother shared their conversation with me, I gasped and murmured. My reaction probably deepened my brother's disdain. I was not offended, but I contributed to his offense. If the truth be told, my flesh enjoyed his outrage because of my feelings for this man, which is why I encouraged his infuriation. Months later, when I looked back at that exchange, I repented for my part in the brother's offense.

Mark 9:42 (NLT) says, "But if you cause one of these little ones who trusts in me to fall into sin, it would be better for you to be thrown into the sea with a large millstone hung around your neck." Offense is a serious issue that destroys destinies. I could have helped that brother to shut the door on his outrage, but instead I fanned it into flames. By God's grace, I will not make that mistake again. We must be careful never to nurture outrage in a fellow believer. Next time someone shares their anger with you, help them to find their way back to love and forgiveness. If they are upset with someone you dislike, choose the high road: guard your mouth, and in so doing, you will help guard their heart.

The Injustice Of Suffering

Offense isn't always directed towards people; sometimes we get upset with God. Hardship may have left you feeling betrayed by the Lord. Perhaps you prayed and believed for the healing of a loved one, but they passed away. Maybe you served God with all your heart, then lost your job. You could have suffered in some other way. Unexpected tragedy can shake you to the core. After our daughter died, I was bewildered. I could not imagine why God had allowed such loss. My husband and I were doing our best pastoring our small but growing church. Why would God allow such a thing?

I never questioned the identity of our daughter's killer (it was the devil). However, I struggled to understand why God had not intervened. I felt like the Lord owed me an explanation, and I believed I could not move forward until He gave me an answer. I was confused and tormented by the questions that spun around my mind. I will never forget the day that the Lord held up a mirror to my heart. I realized that there was no answer that God could give me that would ever be enough. My quest for an explanation trapped me in torment. Led by His Spirit, I knelt down before the Lord and surrendered my right to an answer. I gave up my questions and laid down my confusion as an offering. Soon my peace was restored, and I started my healing journey.

We all go through shocking difficulties. Mark 9:49 (NLT) says, "For everyone will be tested with fire." Learning to lay down any upset with God will help you to make a speedy exit from painful seasons. Although it is never God's desire for His children to be wounded, we need to recognize that anguish is part of life. John 16:1 (AMP) says, "I have told you all these things, so that you should not be offended (taken unawares and falter or be caused to stumble and fall away). [I told you to keep you from being scandalized and repelled.]"

The Way Out

To fulfill your purpose, you need to conquer this destiny blocker, over and over again. Develop a zero-tolerance policy towards even the mildest gripe. There are two keys to obliterating offense. Because you feel wronged when you are offended, first, you need to forgive. Luke 11:4 says, "And forgive us our sins, for we also forgive everyone who is indebted to us..." Offense feels like a debt. You were wronged and someone needs to pay. To be free from this destiny blocker, you need to let go of every upset. You need to give your anger to God as an offering. You need to make the decision that the one who wronged you no longer owes you anything. You need to forgive from the depths of your heart.

The second step will secure your freedom. It will also help to protect you from becoming offended in the future. Mark 4:17 says that we will be easily offended if we have *no real root*. What is the root that guards against offense? In his letter to the church in Ephesus, Paul prayed that God's people would be "...rooted and grounded in love..." (Ephesians 3:17) Love is the root that pulls us back from offense. Ecclesiastes 10:4b (AMP) says: "...gentleness and calmness prevent or put a stop to great offenses." Gentleness is a fruit of the Spirit and an attribute of love.

If you can work out what – or even who – presses your buttons, it will help you to be deliberate about guarding your heart when it might be vulnerable. Who makes you shake your head or causes your blood to boil? What kind of behaviors upset you the most? Which types of people make you feel undermined? Ask God to make you especially gracious around those situations or people. Ask Him to help you to cover the wrongs of others for the sake of your future.

Part of the process of maturing in Christ is learning to love when your flesh wants to be angry. Love is patient when people are unpleasant. It is kind to the uncaring. If someone makes a mistake, love believes the best. It is not easily provoked, even by arrogant or rude behavior. 1 Corinthians 13:5b (AMP) is pertinent: "... Love (God's love in us) does not insist on its own rights or its own way, for it is not self-seeking; it is not touchy or fretful or resentful; it takes no account of the evil done to it [it pays no attention to a suffered wrong]." When we relinquish our rights and choose to be gracious, we choose love. And in the process, we protect our destiny. Love is the antidote to offense. Let's pray.

Heavenly Father,

I want Your highest plans and purposes for my life. I don't want to be shortchanged because of hidden issues. Search my heart, Oh Lord. Shine Your light into the depths of my soul. Reveal any buried offenses. Show me if there is anything that I am holding against anyone, especially if I am offended at somebody in authority. I don't want to harbor any offenses. (*Now sit quietly in God's presence for a few moments and see what He reveals, then continue with the prayer below.*)

I realize that I am holding offenses in my heart. I ask for Your forgiveness, Lord. (*Now tell the Lord who you have been offended at and what they did that caused your anger. Be specific, then continue praying…*) I choose today to get go of all irritation; I give it to You, Lord. I lay down all my anger as an offering; I give it to You. I forgive the person who wronged me. I let go of what they did; I release them. They do not owe me anything. They are free.

Lord, please forgive me for encouraging offense in others. I am sorry for stirring turbulent waters in the hearts of friends or family. I commit today to be an influence for good in the lives of others. I will encourage the people I know to forgive at all times.

Heavenly Father, I ask You to fill me with Your love, especially for those that have let me down. I ask for Your patience and I ask for Your kindness, particularly around people who push my buttons. I will not keep a record of wrongs; they are wiped out, they are cancelled. I choose to be kind and gracious to those who have hurt me. I love others because You love me.

In Jesus' name I pray,

Amen.

WHAT NEXT?

Your heart is probably your most valuable, and yet your most vulnerable, asset. This book is just part of your journey to healing and freedom. As you finish this book, make the decision to continue to prioritize your inner wellbeing. Visit JoNaughton.com to find out about our resources to help you to wholeness. The Heart Academy provides life-changing courses by Zoom on topics like Handling Rejection, Unblocking Your Emotions, and Overcoming Insecurity. We have a mentoring network, online courses, and a range of print, digital, and audio books. We run half day, full day, and two-day events, all designed to help you on your journey. Above all, look after your heart every day of your life, for it determines the course of your life.

"I am convinced and sure of this very thing, that He who began a good work in you will continue until the day of Jesus Christ (right up to the time of His return), developing [that good work] and perfecting and bringing it to full completion in you." (Philippians 1:6 AMP)

Let that word sink deep into you. God is preparing you for your destiny. He has already started the job, and He will be faithful to finish it.

AN INVITATION

If you would like to ask Jesus to become the Lord of your life, I would be honored to lead you in a simple prayer. The Bible says that God loves you and that Jesus wants to draw close to you: "Behold I stand at the door and knock. If anyone hears My voice and opens the door, I will come in." (Revelation 3:20) If you would like to know Jesus as your Friend, your Savior, and your Lord, the first step is to ask. Pray this prayer:

Dear Lord,

I know that You love me and have a wonderful plan for my life. I ask You to come into my heart today and be my Savior and Lord. Forgive me for all my sins, I pray. Thank You that because You died on the cross for me, I am forgiven of every wrong I have ever committed when I repent. I give my life to You entirely and ask You to lead me in Your ways from now on.

In Jesus' name,

Amen.

If you have prayed this prayer for the first time, it will be important to tell a Christian friend what you prayed and to find a good church. Just as a newborn baby needs nourishment and care, so you (and all Christians) need the support of other believers as you start your new life as a follower of Jesus Christ.

You can watch free Bible messages that will help to build your faith by subscribing to my YouTube channel and to Harvest Church London's YouTube channel. You can follow me on Instagram (@naughtonjo), go on Facebook and like my public page (Jo Naughton), and follow me on Twitter (@naughtonjo). God bless you!

ABOUT THE AUTHOR

Jo Naughton is the founder of Whole Heart Ministries, which is dedicated to helping people be free to fulfill their God-given purpose. Together with her husband Paul, Jo pastors Harvest Church in London, England. A public relations executive turned pastor, Jo's previous career included working for King Charles (while he was the Prince) as an executive VP of his largest charity. After reaching the pinnacle of the public relations world, Jo felt the call of God to full-time ministry. She is a regular guest on TV and radio shows in the US and UK.

An international speaker and author, Jo ministers with a heart-piercing anointing, sharing with great personal honesty in conferences and at churches around the world. Her passion is to see people set free from all inner hindrances so that they can fulfill their God-given destiny. Countless people have testified to having received powerful and life-changing healing through her ministry. Jo and Paul have two wonderful children, Ben and Abby.

You can connect with Jo via:

JoNaughton.com

Instagram (@naughtonjo)

YouTube (Jo Naughton)

Facebook (public page – Jo Naughton)

Twitter (@naughtonjo)

For more information about Harvest Church London, visit harvestchurch.org.uk

ALSO BY THE AUTHOR:

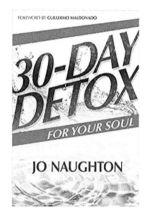

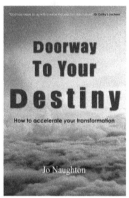

All of Jo Naughton's books are available at: JoNaughton.com

CPSIA information can be obtained
at www.ICGtesting.com
Printed in the USA
LVHW021155080523
746408LV00015B/1534